Advance Praise

Hiring the right leadership coaches to guide an organization comes at a price, often a high one. CEOs who don't understand the myriad benefits that coaching offers may shy away from spending those resources. While many authors are content to have their books rest on store shelves while their readers take a passive approach to reviewing them, Sraban Mukherjee takes a different tactic. As the author cautions, "This book is a TO-DO guide for corporate coaching." So, roll up your sleeves and get ready to dig into this hands-on guide for success! In *Corporate Coaching*, Mukherjee shows how to get an extraordinary return on investment.

—**Dr Marshall Goldsmith**
Bestselling author of *MOJO* and
What Got You Here Won't Get You There

Dr Sraban Mukherjee has advanced the corporate coaching industry with his immanently practical, yet strategically significant, processes, tools, and metrics. As an experienced and certified coach as well as a former human resource executive, Dr Mukherjee is an authority on leadership development and how psychometrics and assessments can be leveraged to evaluate and support coaching engagements. Dr Mukherjee even advises on best practices for building and sustaining internal coaching capabilities and capacity. Sraban's new book is the most complete resource on corporate coaching I have seen to date.

—**John Hoover, PhD**
Co-author of *The Coaching Connection*

A great primer on the coaching field for leaders and coaches in India—and beyond. It is filled with great examples of coaching scenarios. Brings nice clarity to various aspects of the practice, such as the various types of coaching, tools used by coaches, psychometric instruments, and methods of measuring coaching impact.

—Dr Brian O. Underhill
Founder, CoachSource, USA, Co-author,
"Executive Coaching for Results"

Dr Sraban Mukherjee lays out a solid foundation for anyone wanting to learn about coaching. It is highly practical, whilst founded on evidence-based research and his years of being at the top end of coaching.

In this book the reader will find the contemporary positioning of coaching, how to do it, what to expect, and how to give professional standards. It is an excellent book for anyone considering coaching as a career, or who wishes to improve their coaching either internally, in an organization, or who wishes to set up a business as a coach. It is also a good steer for those purchasers of coaching to know how to manage coaches and the coaching process.

—Deborah Tom
Registered Coaching Psychologist, MD, Human Systems, UK

Dr Mukherjee's book is a timely publication that adds to the Indian literature on coaching. It is likely to give the beginners an overview, the experienced more tools, and the thought leaders opportunity to intellectually challenge concepts and experiences. I wish the book all success.

—Dr Santrupt B. Misra
CEO, Carbon Black Business & Director, Group HR,
Aditya Birla Management Corporation Pvt Ltd

Corporate Coaching

Corporate Coaching

The Essential Guide

Sraban Mukherjee, CPC, PCC (ICF)

www.sagepublications.com

Los Angeles • London • New Delhi • Singapore • Washington DC

First published in 2014 by

SAGE Response
B1/I-1 Mohan Cooperative Industrial Area
Mathura Road, New Delhi 110 044, India

SAGE Publications Inc
2455 Teller Road
Thousand Oaks, California 91320, USA

SAGE Publications Ltd
1 Oliver's Yard, 55 City Road
London EC1Y 1SP, United Kingdom

SAGE Publications Asia-Pacific Pte Ltd
3 Church Street
#10-04 Samsung Hub
Singapore 049483

Published by Vivek Mehra for SAGE Publications India Pvt Ltd, Phototypeset in 11/13 Bembo by RECTO Graphics, Delhi and printed at De-Unique, New Delhi.

Library of Congress Cataloging-in-Publication Data

Mukherjee, Sraban, 1956–
  Corporate coaching : the essential guide / by Sraban Mukherjee.
  pages cm
  Includes bibliographical references and index.
  1. Executive coaching. I. Title.
  HD30.4.M847   658.4'07124—dc23   2014   2014001698

ISBN: 978-81-321-1495-6 (PB)

The SAGE Team: Sachin Sharma, Vandana Gupta, Rajib Chatterjee, and Rajinder Kaur

*This book is dedicated to the HR professionals and co-coaches,
who are making difference in the life of every member of the organization
and to those who are in the coaching profession now and
will be in the time to come.*

Thank you for choosing a SAGE product! If you have any comment, observation or feedback, I would like to personally hear from you. Please write to me at <u>contactceo@sagepub.in</u>

—Vivek Mehra, Managing Director and CEO,
SAGE Publications India Pvt Ltd, New Delhi

Bulk Sales

SAGE India offers special discounts for purchase of books in bulk. We also make available special imprints and excerpts from our books on demand.

For orders and enquiries, write to us at

Marketing Department
SAGE Publications India Pvt Ltd
B1/I-1, Mohan Cooperative Industrial Area
Mathura Road, Post Bag 7
New Delhi 110044, India
E-mail us at <u>marketing@sagepub.in</u>

Get to know more about SAGE, be invited to SAGE events, get on our mailing list. Write today to <u>marketing@sagepub.in</u>

This book is also available as an e-book.

Contents

Contents

Foreword

I had the good fortune to meet Dr Sraban Mukherjee back in 2009 on one of my first trips to India. Coaching, I think I can fairly say, was in its infancy in India at that time, with there being a very few if any International Coach Federation certified coaches, but lots of people calling themselves coaches. There was a type of "wild west" feel about coaching at the time with everyone and everything vying for an early credibility in a wide open market.

What you hold in your hands here is no small feat. Sraban has taken his trained academic mind and created essentially an encyclopedia (or should I say Wikipedia now?) of corporate coaching. This book provides a comprehensive guide for anyone who needs to know the ins and outs of corporate coaching, when to use it, how to use it and the many variations of coaching, assessments, and other tools.

This book is a must read for those who are charged with creating and implementing a successful and measurable corporate coaching program. It is also a useful guide to distinguish among the many hundreds of coaches out there claiming to be experts, by giving insight into the quite a few of the different schools of thought of coaching.

Finally, I think that Sraban has done a tremendous service to the field of coaching by writing this very practical book. He clearly shifts the attitude around coaching to one of a positive development tool versus a tool used to "fix" leaders. With this book, corporate leaders in India have cases and practical examples of how to use coaching to their company's best advantage.

As India's use of corporate coaching grows, those who have read this book will be at a distinct advantage. And I imagine Sraban will no doubt be challenging certain edges of the frontier even then …

.

Keep this book on the edge of your desk. You'll find it amazingly useful.

Libby Robinson, MCC (ICF)
MA Organizational Development & Transformation
Managing Partner, Integral Leadership and Coaching, Paris

Preface

I spent around three decades in large organizations at various roles and was actively involved in developmental human resource function, wherein my major role was continuously reengineering executive development programs in order to build leadership pipeline in continual and sustainable basis. I am personally involved in coaching profession, mainly in executive and leadership coaching, for last 10 years. Over this period, I realized that many developmental HR initiatives undertaken in organizations (including myself when I was heading Human Resource function) were based on developmental needs or on bridging the competency gaps of the executives. However, these were not as effective as should have been.

This has compelled me to write a book on a different paradigm on coaching, popularly known as positive psychology. I have seen many executives, whether at front line or profit center head position, irrespective of whether they are from brick and mortar companies or financial sector or service industries or not-for-profit organizations, have made significant progress in their professional and personal life when they have been exposed to coaching. Majority of organizations, that have introduced coaching as developmental interventions, are focusing on executive coaching for a selective few individuals and that also not on regular basis for various reasons. Hence, my intention is to help a large number of executives, working at various organizations, who can get exposed to coaching to make progress in their career as well as make them more effective in their profession.

My primary objective of writing this book is to present a comprehensive approach on how coaching can be helpful for all levels of management to improve their personal effectiveness, which in turn impacts organizational performance. Hence, this book on corporate coaching not only covers executive coaching but also includes the other powerful coaching domain, viz., behavioral coaching, performance coaching, coaching for talent development and leadership coaching. This book also covers how to build the coaching capabilities within the organization through internal coaching, which in turn helps in developing coaching culture in the organization. This book looks at various relevant theories, processes, techniques and the tools available to the coaching domain.

Over the last decade, there are considerable researches in coaching on theory, strategy, practice, and application. I am also involved actively in action research areas of coaching. This book quotes from some of my reviewed research papers related to corporate coaching, while discussing specific genre of coaching practices. During the last five years, I have conducted several coaching skill workshops for various organizations and around thousand managers, mostly as departmental or functional heads, have attended these workshops. This book covers some of my learnings on how coaching can be effectively used in routine performance challenges of organizations.

This book is a TO-DO guide for corporate coaching. Hence, a lot of emphasis has been given on performing aspects of coaching by giving hands-on tips and case scenarios. Several caselets of coaching scenario that I have encountered in the course of coaching practice in corporate sector in India have been presented, so that the readers are able to correlate with similar coaching challenges they face in their organizations.

This book mentions coach as a person, who is hired from outside the organization, to deliver coaching to an executive, who may be at any level of management. The coach and the executive may be of any gender. If this book refers, in some places, to male executive or male coach, it also implies to female coach and/or female executive. The coach in some situations may be internal coach also. The words "employee," "executive," and "coachee" are used interchangeably throughout this book, but it means primarily employee(s) of corporations, whether for profit or non-profit in nature.

Audience for This Book

This book is targeted primarily for senior HR/L&D professionals and CEOs/COOs of organizations, who are considering to introduce coaching for their executives. This book will help them to make decisions on which specific coaching, viz., leadership coaching or executive coaching or performance coaching or coaching for talent management or behavioral coaching, will be useful for their target executive or group of executives. This book will help them to understand how coaching can help their executives, how to choose the right coach, how the coaching process works and what are the roles they need to play in the process. This book also helps the top management or decision makers of coaching intervention on how to evaluate the return of coaching investment, direct or indirect.

This book will be helpful for those coaches who have just started coaching in organizations. This book will help them to get into the details of the processes, methodologies, and theories associated with corporate coaching practice. This book will work as a resource book for corporate coaches, in terms of advanced coaching tools, psychological inventories and its applications.

This book will also help those executives who are just introduced into coaching. They will know what coaching is all about and what to expect in coaching journey. This book will also be useful to leaders, who are contemplating to get into coaching, but not sure how coaching will help them in improving their managerial and leadership capabilities.

Overview of the Contents

Chapter 1 focuses on coaching basics. It covers "what is coaching," "what is not coaching" and different niches of coaching. It then defines "what is corporate coaching" and why corporate coaching is beneficial not only for its employees' growth but also for overall organizational performance improvement.

Chapters 2–6 cover the model, strategies, processes, and methodologies of executive coaching, behavioral coaching, performance coaching, leadership coaching, and coaching for talent development. Each chapter covers a detailed roadmap of implementation, so that all stakeholders of coaching get clear understanding of their roles at various stages of coaching journey. Several coaching case-studies, supporting information, sample charts and formats are added to help the readers to understand the coaching process.

Chapter 7 discusses the development of coaching capabilities within the organization using internal coaching. This chapter dealt with the pros and cons of this intervention, the processes of development of internal coaches and how to make the process effective. It also covers how coaching skill development program is to be designed.

Chapters 8–10 cover different coaching tools and inventories. Chapter 8 covers some of the advanced coaching tools, which must be in the toolkit of corporate coaches. Chapter 9 covers some of the important psychological and psychometric tools used in corporate coaching domain. This chapter introduces each tool on how to interpret these inventories and the potential areas of application. Chapter 10 covers 360-degree assessment tool for coaching needs' identification. Besides presenting different aspects of designing and using 360-degree assessment tools, this chapter discusses in detail the two most popular 360-degree assessment tools, namely, LSI and EQ 360.

Chapter 11 covers how to measure the effectiveness of coaching intervention. Since, every coaching intervention requires high investment in terms of cost and time, it is important for organizational leaders to assess the return of such high investment.

Acknowledgments

This book is the culmination of my long years of experience of working in various corporations in human resource function and then taking up coaching as a profession. During my initial phase of coaching career, I came across several books on coaching, did lots of browsing on Internet and went through various research journals to get myself fully equipped on what works and what does not work. I also understood how to address challenges of corporations in coaching interventions and what differentiates coaching intervention in the organizations from the other developmental strategies. Unfortunately, the process was long, tedious but not of much of use. Then I started discussion with my coaching mentors on the challenges faced by majority of executives in corporations as they struggle to navigate their path in highly complex, polarized, chaotic and uncertain environment. Sheri Boone and Jim Clarkson are two of my mentors, who have always provided me new insights on coaching within an organization.

I am deeply inspired by the seminal work of Dr Marshall Goldsmith and Sir John Whitmore. I believe their contributions in coaching are immense and all coaches get insights on how to address the critical issues of coaching corporate clients. I am also influenced by the work of Martin Seligman and Mithaly Csikszentmihalyi on positive psychology, which is reflected significantly throughout this book.

I owe gratitude to Prabha, Vijay, Madhav, and Tapas, who were some of my initial corporate coaching clients. They gave me different perspectives and new insights. I owe my gratitude to Oil and Natural Gas Corporation (a large public sector enterprise in India), where I was involved in large-scale deployment of internal coaching program. The participants of this program (i.e., manager-coaches) have sown a seed of enquiry in me about what corporate coaching is all about and distinguishing it from other niche of coaching. I am also indebted to *International Journal of Coaching in Organization, International Journal of Mentoring* and *Coaching and International Journal of Evidence-based Coaching and Mentoring* for publishing my action-research papers, which reinforced some of the thesis on coaching.

My deepest gratitude is to all men and women from various organizations, multinational to national corporations, large to small, profit to not-for profit, who have shared their experiences, stories, challenges and dilemmas, while undergoing coaching conversation with me.

I am grateful to Libby Robinson for writing the Foreword of this book. She was the first person with whom I shared my idea on writing a book in this domain a few years back. Deep gratitude is expressed for Dr Marshall Goldsmith, Dr John Hoover, Dr Santrup Mishra, Deborah Tom, and Dr Brian O. Underhill for going through the thick manuscript in spite of their busy schedule and providing me their valuable inputs as well as endorsements for this book. It really meant a lot to me personally. I am also thankful to my good friend Dr Gopal Mahapatra for encouraging me to write the book on this subject and sharing his experiences.

I am thankful to SAGE publications for agreeing to publish this book. In particular, I am thankful to R. Chandrasekhar, Associate Vice President, Commissioning, who happens to be my key contact for my earlier book also.

Finally, I am grateful to my parents for sharing their compassion and affection, to my wife, Urmi, for encouragement and support and my son, Neil, for pursing his quest for excellence.

CHAPTER 1

Overview of Corporate Coaching

Coaching is the fastest growing profession in the world today. Its origin can be traced back to Aristotle, Socrates, the Gestalt theory, and ontology. Coaching is a distinct process of helping people to fulfill their dreams and aspirations and create a better life for themselves. Though it appeared in different forms till the early 1990s, it only flourished much later. Coaching draws upon a wide range of influences from various disciplines, viz., psychology, philosophy, sports, spirituality, behavioral science, psychotherapy, counseling, ontology, and management development.

Ten years back, no one in corporate India was paying serious attention to coaching, though the concept of mentoring was very much in practice in Indian organizations. However during the last decade, coaching became a well-established profession in developed countries such as United States, Canada, some parts of Europe and Asia-Pacific countries, namely, Australia, New Zealand, and Singapore. As it was reported a few years back, 69 percent corporations in USA were using the services of executive coaching and more than 10,000 executive coaches were practicing in USA alone. International Coach Federation (ICF), having its headquarter in USA, is the largest association of coaches. It had around 19,000 professional coaches as members from different parts of the world in 2011. Association for Coaching (AC) and European Mentoring and Coaching Council (EMCC) are some other leading coaching associations, based in Europe. These two associations had more than 5,000 coaches and mentors in 2011. There are other associations of coaches such as Worldwide Association of Business Coaches (WABC), The International Association of Coaching (IAC), International Institute of Coaching (IIC), Asia-Pacific Association of Coaches, etc., actively involved in coaching.

Around five years back (i.e., 2006–2007), when if I had mentioned to anyone that I am a coach, the next question they would have asked me is what type of coaching business I am in. Knowing very well what they were hinting at, I would have said, I don't conduct coaching classes for students aspiring for admission to technical colleges. Their next response would have been generally, "Oh! You are coaching budding sportspersons." They would have further asked me then which type of sport I am giving coaching. In India, cricket is considered as one sort of religion. Here, every parent expects their child to be a Sachin Tendulkar in the future. Hence, they are always looking for a good cricket coaching school or a good cricket coach. I would have politely replied that "I am a corporate coach," hence nothing to do with sports coaching as such. They finally would have got disappointed and asked me, "what is that?"

Being in human resource profession for almost two decades, the story was not much different with my corporate peers. I was working with a consulting and training company in the National Capital Region of Delhi. Obviously when I joined that organization (during 2005 and 2006), many colleagues from the training division were introducing themselves as Voice Coaches (they were actually trainers for BPO employees). During the initial phase of my induction in the organization, some of them asked me what I was delivering different in corporate coaching than what they were actually doing in the BPO sector. Due to my limited knowledge of BPO industry at that time, I asked one such trainer "How do you coach BPO employees?" She replied, "Well, I listen to the calls made by an associate a couple of times, and then I point out to the associate the mistakes made by him/her and the potential loss of the sales lead which had taken place due to that." Well, in my mind, I thought this is just negative feedback, neither coaching nor even counseling. In organizations (mostly Indian), I might have spent hours, during the early 2000s, to explain to some senior human resource professionals that coaching and mentoring are not the same interventions, even though both the terms "coaching" and "mentoring" are used interchangeably in some organizations.

Another interesting point of view that I encountered once from one of my knowledgeable friends in the corporate world (who always introduces himself as Coach) is that coaching is used as a tool for performance improvement in sports now being introduced in organizations to improve the poor performance of employees, by quoting from Sir John Whitmore's book *Coaching for performance* and Timothy Galley's book *Inner game of tennis*. It is an absolutely wrong concept of coaching. Sir John Whitmore actually defined coaching as "unlocking a person's potential to maximize their performance." He never mentioned that coaching is only meant for poor performers. However, the scenario is quite different now (say, from 2009 onwards). Coaching has become one of the emerging thrust areas for human resource development function in corporate India.

How Coaching Helps in Improving Organizational Effectiveness

The role of managers, within an organization, is deploying limited resources to get the job done efficiently. The "command and control" approach or "telling people what to do and how to do" of managing people is not appropriate nowadays in organizations. In command and control culture, also called as top-down culture, the employees, in general, do not feel valued or recognized. The characteristics of such organizations are weak in proactiveness, poor interpersonal communication, and high reaction time to external demands. Though we find the emergence of "flat structure," "matrix organization," "virtual organization," and "cross-functional team," etc., it is still not uncommon to find "command and control" style in management within many organizations, which resulted in low employee motivation, less empowerment at the operating level, high employee turnover and low employee productivity. The organizational leaders have started realizing during the last two decades that organizations are not only like machines or systems and processes, but rather it is a collection of individuals and human beings with dreams, aspirations, and expectations. Hence traditional human resource processes, systems, and tools are not sufficiently geared up to address the expectations of all employees to a large extent.

The high-performing organizations have also realized that talent and human capital are the key differentiators between their organization and the rest of other organizations. The ability of an organization to learn faster than their competitors gives only sustainable competitive advantage in the long run. The war for talent is a never-ending reality in a high-performing organization. In the era of downsizing, managers are promoted much faster to senior executive positions at a very young age to handle much bigger roles in a flat organization structure. This has resulted in lack of requisite skills amongst these managers. Creative ways of retaining and inspiring talented employees are being found in the era of downsizing, reengineering, merger, and acquisition. Competencies that proved to be highly effective in the past have become outdated and new competencies need to be acquired much faster to face the present-day realities and challenges.

There is growing interest in large Indian corporations to use coaching in leadership capability development initiatives. Coaching is about nurturing potential leaders within an organization and hence organizations are using coaching to sharpen the skills of individuals who have been identified as future organizational leaders. Organization realizes that skills and knowledge of employees are not enough to bring about any outstanding performance. Thus, there is an urgent need to create a motivating environment so that the individual employee takes personal responsibility and ownership for improving one's performance while maintaining focus on the organization's goals. Organizations are transforming it into a learning organization, where the employees are praised, encouraged, involved, and empowered by delegating responsibility with authority. In this context, coaching is being deployed to transform leaders, managers, teams, and the entire organization from good to great for enhancement of the organizational performance by strengthening its essential competitive advantage: Its people.

Indian organizations are now allocating higher budget in training and employee development activities, since organizations are beginning to realize that the soft skills/competencies such as "coaching and mentoring," "development of subordinates," "people management," "interpersonal relations," "networking," etc., are equally important skills as the technical or operational skills/competencies. Most of the large corporations have developed competency framework for leadership and managerial levels. They have conducted assessment centers for their leaders and managers to identify developmental needs based on the gap identified in the competencies they should have as per the organizational competency framework. It is not very uncommon to notice that, "coaching" is one of the skills/competencies that always occupy a prominent place in the list of competencies, which most of the senior managers are lacking.

Coaching is about moving executives from dependence to interdependence and seeing them through a Situational Leadership Journey, which raises their levels of commitment and competence to a point where the executives no longer need the direct guidance of their seniors. The Situational Leadership model of Blanchard and Hersey suggests that competent and committed people are the ones to benefit the most from coaching since they already possess major knowledge and skills.

Some organizations are putting more focus on "coaching" to ensure that their managers coach their employees. But even with this new emphasis, development and actual implementation of coaching skill within organizations is widely varied. Those organizations that valued the development of these types of skills/competencies previously are well ahead of the game, whereas many organizations are still struggling on how to proceed.

The major reasons for which organizations are going for coaching are as follows:

- Developing executives, mostly senior executives, is a challenge since these executives are having difficulties in getting feedback, acknowledging the need for change and adapting new behavior, which is crucial for their effectiveness in a new role.

- Group training or public training, having participants at different hierarchical levels, inhibits and restricts senior executives to participate fully or open up, resulting in losing the much desired benefits from such investment.

- After the managers undergo specific skill training or get exposed to new technology, the managers encounter major hurdles during implementation of new skills in their workplace. Coaching supports the managers to implement new skills as per their individual learning style at their own pace and internalize the learning.

- Coaching helps executives, who are in career transition to leadership position, in acquiring new behavior and improving dysfunctional behavior.

Then, What Is the Meaning of Coaching?

The ICF defines coaching as partnering with coachees in a thought-provoking and creative process that inspires them to maximize their personal and professional potential. Coaching honors the coachee as the expert in his/her life and work and believes that every coachee is creative, resourceful and whole. Standing on these foundations, the coach's responsibility is to:

- Discover, clarify, and align with what the coachee wants to achieve;
- Encourage coachee self-discovery;

- Elicit coachee-generated solutions and strategies; and
- Hold the coachee responsible and accountable.

Timothy Gallwey, Harvard educationalist and tennis expert, defined coaching as, "Coaching is unlocking a person's potential to maximize their own performance. It is helping them to learn rather than teaching them." Coaching is more focused on helping coachee (employee) to learn and releasing his/her potential. Socrates had voiced the same things some 2000 years earlier, but we have forgotten his philosophy in corporations for many generations.

Witherspoon and White (1997) point out that the root meaning of the verb "to coach" is to convey a valued person from where one was to where one wants to be—such as an actual coach or carriage would take a passenger on a journey. Coaching is a conversation about the future, rather than the past. Hence, the coach works together with the coachee toward a compelling future, which pulls them forward into action. Professional coaches provide an ongoing partnership that is designed to help the coachees produce fulfilling results in their personal and professional lives. Coaches help the coachees improve their performances and enhance the quality of their lives.

Coaches are trained to listen, to observe, and to customize their approach to individual coachee needs. They seek to elicit solutions and strategies from the coachee; they believe that the coachee is naturally creative and resourceful. The coach's job is to provide support to enhance the skills, resources, and creativity that the coachee already has.

One way to understand what coaching is to rule out what it is not.

Coaching Is Not Mentoring

The coaching profession struggles to differentiate its offerings from that of mentoring, since the interpretations of the concept vary largely between these two professions. Mentoring is basically a system of semi-structured guidance whereby one person shares his/ her knowledge, skills, and experiences to assist others to progress in their own lives and careers. Mentoring is a directive process between a senior person (mentor) with knowledge or experience or skill in a given field and a junior employee (mentee). A coach is generally not from the same organization, but is hired from outside to support an employee, generally from middle to senior level, while a mentor is from within the organization.

There are two types of assistance that mentors provide to their mentees. The first assistance is for their career aspirations, which directly aid the mentees in career advancement. This includes exposure, protection, sponsorship, skills, knowledge, and providing challenging opportunities. The second type of assistance is more of psychological support, which includes acceptance, confirmation, counseling, role modeling, friendship as well as giving guidance.

Many large organizations, in both public and private sectors including multi-national organizations, have well-structured mentoring schemes wherein new entrants such as graduate engineering trainees, management trainees, etc., are assigned with a mentor, generally a senior person, who provides professional and organizational know-how, career support, and assistance during their initial phase of induction in the organization. However, coaching relationship is a partnership whereby the coach walks side by side with the coachee. The following points broadly distinguish coaching from mentoring.

COACHING

- Coaches seldom mentor.
- Coaches help the coachee/employee to decide what they want to do.
- Coaching focuses on a specific performance or behavioral issue.
- Coaches teach how to complete a specific step in a process.

- A coaching relationship is usually over when performance gets better or improved.
- "Coaching" is an event.

MENTORING

- Mentors could be coaches.
- Mentoring focuses on overall development of the mentee/employee.
- Mentors teach the mentee/employee how to complete the overall process.
- A mentoring relationship unfolds and strengthens over time and is usually for a longer term.
- "Mentoring" is a journey.

Coaching Is Not Training

Most conventional training and development activities within an organization focus on teaching specific knowledge and skills, what employees need, to perform their task. Hence, training is a teacher-centered approach, deployed for improvement of knowledge or skills for which there is a performance gap. Coaching, on the other hand, is an employee-centered approach that is most suitable to address performance gaps that are to do with lack of motivation or lack of commitment.

Classroom trainers, generally, carry out training activity for a group of employees on a predefined course module designed based on the program objectives. During training, the trainers transfer the knowledge and skills to employees using the "telling and instructing" approach. The trainer is assumed to be master on the subjects and have more knowledge and skills than the trainees. However, coaching is a coachee-centered approach and coaches believe that the coachees/employees are the experts in their field.

Coaching Is Not Consulting

A consultant usually is an expert in a given area. They are hired for their expertise to give recommendations for solving a particular problem the individual is facing. Once the problem is solved, the role of the consultant ceases. Usually, consultants do not get involved in areas beyond their areas of specialization.

Coaching, however, uses a more holistic approach. The coach, along with the coachee, examines the problem, creates a plan of action, and works side by side with the coachee during implementation of the solution. The coach is not an expert in the business of the coachee. The coach does not have the answers for the problems the coachee is facing. The coach collaborates with the coachee to create a solution using the coachee's knowledge and expertise.

Counseling Is Not Coaching

Counseling is a highly skilled intervention focused on helping individuals address psycho-social and work-related performance problems. Counseling is a solution-focused intervention, which implies that there is a problem for which a solution needs to be found to avoid reoccurrence. It is based on the past and focuses on fixing a work-related problem of the coachee/employee. The role of counselor is to understand the root cause of long-standing performance problems/issues at work and find a solution for the coachee/employee. The relationship between counselor and coachee/employee is always hierarchical.

Coaching, on the other hand, begins with the present and assists the coachee/employee in setting goals that he/she wants to achieve in the future. In coaching, discussion about the past with the coachee/employee is only to discover what is blocking them from moving forward. Coaches are not necessarily experts but more of a person with a set of skills they use to support the coachee to achieve their goals. Coaching relationship is present- and future-based action oriented and not hierarchical in nature.

Psychotherapy Is Not Coaching

Psychotherapy focuses on issues of pathology, healing, and unresolved psychological issues of the past. Though both coaching and psychotherapy deal with behavior, emotion, and cognition, corporate coaches have a broader perspective than the psychotherapist. Corporate coaches are expected to know the intricacies of management, understanding of the overall organizational context of the coachee and the organization, in general. While in psychotherapy, information is principally taken from the individual, in coaching, coaches gather information not only from the coachee but also from all the stakeholders with whom the coachee might have dealings during the coaching process. Psychotherapy tends to be past-, present-, and future-oriented while coaching has a more present and future orientation. In coaching there is a goal and action orientation, whereas the psychotherapy process is more passive and reflective.

The primary interest area of psychotherapy is symptom reduction and character problems, while in coaching the focus is on personal growth and self-development. While coaching conversation can take place in the form of face-to-face meeting, email, telephonic conversation, or group session, the psychotherapy sessions are generally conducted in the therapist's office.

A psychotherapist works with a dysfunctional person to make him functional. Therapists generally work with the people who need help to become emotionally healthy. They often deal with past issues and devise ways to overcome them. Psychotherapy also tends to focus on feelings and experiences related to past events.

A coach works with a functional person to help them in order to become a magnificent person. Coaching does not generally rely much on past issues of the coachee but rather focuses on where the coachee is right now and from there, where they want to go and how to overcome the differences. Coaching is oriented toward goal setting and encourages the coachee to move forward.

Let us now briefly discuss the different types of coaching that are commonly being offered. There are several niche areas in coaching. However, the most popular coaching niches are discussed in the following sections.

PERSONAL/LIFE COACHING

Grant (2001) defined life coaching as a solution-focused, result-oriented systematic process in which the coach facilitates the enhancement of the coachee's life experience and performance in various domains (as determined by the coachee), and fosters the self-directed learning and personal growth of the coachee.

The personal/life coach helps individuals gain awareness and clarity of their personal goals and priorities, have a better understanding of their thoughts, feelings, and options, and take appropriate actions to change their lives, accomplish their goals, and feel more fulfilled. It involves clarifying values and visions, setting life goals, and preparing actions toward achieving their visions, goals, and desires and bringing life-transforming experiences.

Life coaching normally takes place at the behest of an individual who wants some help in resolving issues in his/her personal life. These issues could be ranging from relationship issues to tackling significant turning points in the life of the coachee.

CAREER COACHING

Career coaching has experienced an explosive growth in recent years. Career coaching is all about equipping individuals with practical guidance on how to move up, across in the organization, or into a completely new field altogether.

Career coaching helps individuals identify what they want and expect from their career, what are the options available to make decisions of their career choices, and to take actions needed to accomplish their career objectives in balance with the other parts of their lives. The coachees for career coaching generally bring the following issues for coaching:

- Which career direction is right for me?
- Should I stay in this job, or find another one?
- Which job offer should I take?
- Which career-building assignments should I be pursuing to fast-track my career?
- When should I take that career break or when I should take a big career decision?
- Whether I should take up corporate job or not?
- Am I ready for career transition?
- How to deal with expectations of employers?
- Whether I should leave job and start entrepreneurial activity?

SPIRITUAL COACHING OR TRANSPERSONAL COACHING

Spiritual coaching taps into the power center of both within the coachee and within the coach. Any coachee with any agenda can be coached with a spiritual style, whether the coachee is a profit center head trying to improve their profit margins or a parent talking about challenges with their teenage kids. A spiritual coach is likely to coach with intuition as their default mode.

Spiritual coaching tries to harness the transformative power of "spirit" so that the coachee is in touch with the "inner self" and gets its guidance. Instead of focusing on external factors of life, a spiritual coach focuses on the inner workings of the coachee's mind, body, and soul. A spiritual coach takes the help of spiritual principles and spiritual ideals into the coaching discussion to help the coachee overcome life's troubles. A spiritual coach also assists the coachee to live from consciousness so that the coachee can live a complete life. A spiritual coach helps his/her coachees to improve certain areas of their life, such as determining their spiritual path, how to proceed on their spiritual journey, and how to shrug off the negative events that seem to occur daily.

BUSINESS COACHING

People come to business coaches for two reasons: inspiration and desperation.

- *Inspired* people want a coach to help them do better.
- *Desperate* people want a coach to help them get out of a jam-like situation.

The entry point in business coaching is usually a business issue. The coachee may want to increase sales, promote better teamwork, enhance productivity, reduce turnover, or improve quality. But the coaching relationship, once initiated, invariably moves beyond the initial perceived needs of "fix my business," "expanding business," "arranging finance," etc., gradually and naturally into "fix me."

Business coaching can be applied to all types of businesses. Business coaching is generally useful for entrepreneurs, owners, or managers of small companies, start-up companies, professionals in private practice, individuals running business from their homes, and someone who wishes to start one's own enterprise. Business coaches help the business owners/managers in small-scale organizations develop, promote, and grow their businesses, and upgrade their employees as well as themselves.

WELLNESS COACHING

Wellness coaching helps individuals improve all areas of wellness including fitness, nutrition, weight, stress, health, and management of the life issues that impact wellness. The wellness coaching field is fairly new, and began in the late 1990s. A wellness coach works with coachees to encourage them to change certain aspects of their lives that are unhealthy. This could include changing dietary habits, changing lifestyles, going for fitness exercises/program, quitting smoking, etc. Wellness coaching also focuses on the behavioral change that needs to occur.

The wellness coaching skills can be applied to all types of sport coaching, fitness coaching as well as health coaching. The sports coaches not only teach the coachees the specific skills but also guide them on specific lifestyles, diet plan, and workout besides keeping them motivated. A naturopath can tell people what to eat but also the need to understand what might have caused health problems in the first place. Wellness coaches are highly sought-after professionals, as today's health-conscious generation focuses on prevention and work-life balance instead of on traditional solutions.

EXECUTIVE COACHING

Executive coaching is an experiential and individualized executive development process that builds an executive's capability to achieve short- and long-term organizational goals. It is conducted through one-to-one interactions, driven by data from multiple perspectives and based on mutual trust and respect. The organization, an executive, and the executive coach, all work in partnership to achieve maximum impact (www.executivecoachingforum.com, third edition, January 2004, p. 19). The following two factors always distinguish executive coaching from other types of coaching:

1. Executive coaching involves a partnership among executive, coach, and organization.
2. The individual goals of an executive coaching engagement must always link back and be subordinated to strategic organizational objectives.

ONTOLOGICAL COACHING

Ontology is the study of being. In ontological coaching, the coach observes and works with key aspects of how coachee have structured their reality and the nature of their existence so that the coach is able to develop a sound understanding of what aspects of the coachee's way of being, are generating an unhelpful reality and support the coachee to develop a more constructive reality that will lead to positive changes in the coachee's world.

The ontological approach in coaching enables the coach to observe and work constructively with three essential domains of human existence, i.e., language, emotions, and body. The ontological coach becomes an acute observer of how:

1. The coachee uses language;
2. The emotional experiences of the coachee; and
3. The particular ways of language and emotion are configured in the coachee's body.

The role of the coach is to respectfully inquire with the coachee about how shifts can occur in each domain of language, emotions, and body, to generate constructive new perspectives that open new possibilities for effective action by the coachee (Sieler, Alan, *Ontology: A theoretical basis for professional coaching*, www. paracomm. com/articles/onlogy.html).

BEHAVIORAL COACHING

The goal of behavioral coaching is to effect sustained change in an executive's behavior that improves performance. However, any behavior change occurs over a period of time. Behavioral coach assists the coachees to practice new behavior in a structured way and supports them during the change process so that the coachee does not revert to the old behavior.

Behavioral coaching, as defined by Skiffington and Zeus (2003), is a structured, process-driven relationship between a trained professional coach and an individual or team, which includes assessment, examining values and motivation, setting measurable goals, defining focused action plans, and using validated tools and techniques to help coachees develop competencies and remove blocks to achieve valuable and sustainable changes in their personal and professional lives.

LEADERSHIP COACHING

Leadership coaching is useful for those individuals who are being groomed for promotion or just promoted to leadership position. The goal of leadership coaching is to clarify with the leader as to what are the key constituents of their new role, the important responsibilities and deliverables in the first few months, and how to integrate the team they will be leading.

Leadership coaching mainly focuses on development of leadership competencies, viz., developing and communicating strategic vision, strategic planning, driving cultural change initiatives, ambassadorship, leading executive teams, overcoming isolation, interpersonal skills, communication, dealing effectively with colleagues, etc. Leadership coaching is often initiated for large-scale leadership capability development interventions, enhancing performance levels of high-potential managers as well as aligning organizational goals and targets with that of individuals.

There are a lot of commonalities between executive coaching and leadership coaching niche, since both these terms are used interchangeably by coaching practitioners. Broadly speaking, executive coaching is applicable for the population of N or N-1 managers, i.e., functional heads or departmental heads levels. Leadership coaching is offered to a broader population: all those who want to grow in leadership or want to gain more awareness on the effects they generate while leading others.

PERFORMANCE COACHING

Performance coaching is a step-by-step process, which, through skilful questioning, active listening, and staying on the coachee's agenda, helps the executives, managers, and employees improve their performance and productivity, by encouraging commitment and promoting a climate of motivation.

Performance coaches help employees at all levels to understand if there is any gap in their current performance and opportunities to improve their performance. Coaches help the employees understand the requirements of their jobs and the competencies needed to perform their role.

Generally, performance coaching tools are a very useful resource for managers, which help them develop strategies for their team to improve performance by focusing on the gap and develop strategies for improving performance by exploiting opportunities in keeping the coachee/employees engaged, motivated, and focused.

DEVELOPMENTAL COACHING

Developmental coaches work with the high-potential managers, identified by talent management process or succession planning process of the organization, to develop key competencies. The coach works with the organization to develop the potential of individuals who have been identified as a key resource to the organization's future or are part of the organization's succession plan. Generally, organizations use the assessment center approach to identify the competency gap and develop individual development plans based on the assessment results. Developmental coach works with the coachee to improve the identified competencies through a structured process of developmental coaching.

SUCCESSION COACHING

Succession coaching helps organizations assess potential candidates for senior management or leadership positions and prepares them for promotion to more senior roles. This is done whenever these positions are to be filled up internally due to separation or superannuation of the present incumbent. In this type of coaching, assessment of employees and preparation of development plan are prerequisites, before starting the coaching process.

TEAM COACHING

Team coaches work with the leader and members of a team to establish the team mission, team strategies, and rules of engagement with each other. The team coaches then work with the team collectively to develop team goals, plan of actions, and defining the role each member has to play to achieve team goals. The team leader and member may be coached individually or collectively to facilitate the team members on how to enhance team effectiveness to achieve team goals.

Corporate Coaching: What It Is and How It Can Be Used?

Let us start with the concept of coaching as it is today in most organizations. Professional coaches are being brought inside the organization usually only for individuals at a more senior level within the organization. The coaching intervention is generally focused on addressing a performance issue or preparing someone for a specific role. The "coach" in these cases is usually a professional from outside, who is skilled and trained in coaching skills with relevant coaching experience. Corporate human resource department is only interested in hiring the services of external executive coaches for a selected few senior managers, since hiring an external coach is quite expensive. Though the number of executive coaching opportunities is limited within an organization, high compensation makes executive coaching an attractive profession. This may be the reason we see more number of executive coaches (at least in India, and may be true for many countries including EU countries) than life or career coaches.

To me, executive coaching is one of the opportunities for an individual at a senior level to improve self-awareness and achieve success in a business context with the support of a coach. The exciting changes come when the skills learnt through this process become ingrained and applied to bigger, global issues where individuals go "beyond" themselves using a leadership approach. Hence leadership coaching becomes more important for those who would like to develop authentic leadership styles and behavior. When an employee grows within the organization, either horizontally or vertically, it becomes essential for the employee to acquire new skills and competencies, for being effective in the new role. Developmental coaching helps them acquire new skills and competencies as per their own individual needs and learning styles.

When any senior executive moves from a functional role to a profit center role, he/she needs the support of a business coach to navigate the personal change journey. In large organizations, it is impossible to bring a large number of external coaches for large-scale organization development initiative or cultural change. Internal coaching initiative, wherein managers are trained to be coaches, is most effective for the development of a large number of managerial resources through the coaching "ripple through" effect within the organization. When an organization needs breakthrough performance or a particular team or teams need to enhance performance significantly, performance coaching is the most powerful tool for managers to improve team performance or productivity. When leaders and high-performing managers become ineffective in managing their team due to their dysfunctional behaviors, behavioral coaches assist these managers in discarding dysfunctional behaviors and acquiring new effective behaviors for their present role.

Hence, corporate coaching encompasses executive coaching, leadership coaching, business coaching, performance coaching, ontological coaching, performance coaching, career coaching, internal coaching, developmental coaching, succession coaching, and team coaching for different levels of employees to address different developmental needs in order to create a high-performing organization through sustainable and continuous employee development efforts. Corporate coaching can be used for a variety of purposes from enhancing specific leadership skills, to creating effective teams, to assisting key managers in setting priorities, to helping executives balance work-life concerns and to maximizing performance to assist executives in transition. The purpose of corporate coaching is to make highly effective people even more effective, but not to make weak executives or low-performing executives improve their performance. Corporate coaching helps executives polish their existing rough edges.

Corporate coaching has various forms of delivery. The most prevalent formats of corporate coaching are one-on-one coaching, shadow coaching, and group or team coaching. In shadow coaching, the corporate coach follows the executives at their workplace, including attending review meeting, staff meeting, or customer meeting and gives them feedback based on what is observed. In team coaching, the coach assists all the members of the team collectively to enhance the team performance and achieve the team goals.

Chapter Summary

After globalization and opening of Indian economy during the 1990s, many organizations have started facing stiff challenges and competitions. And, therefore, today to survive in the market, one has to keep oneself ahead of others in every respect. For this purpose, we need outstanding performances from managers in deploying limited resources judiciously, so as to get the job done most efficiently. Thus, there is an urgent need to create a motivating environment so that an individual employee takes personal responsibility and ownership for improving one's own performance.

In this regard, the organization has to take care of two factors, i.e., talent and human capital; which are the main differentiating factors between two organizations. It is also seen that in the present scenario, the traditional human resource processes, systems, tools, etc., are not sufficiently geared up to address the expectations of individual employees or of the team to achieve breakthrough performance to face the challenges today. Also, the competencies that proved to be effective in the past have become outdated and, therefore, new competencies need to be acquired much faster to face the present day's competition and challenges.

In this regard corporate coaching has come to play a significant role in overcoming the above challenges. Basically coaching is unlocking a person's potential to maximize his/her own performance. It is concerned about the future rather than the past. It focuses on where the employee is right now and from there where he/she wants to go and how to overcome the differences. Basically coaching uses a more holistic approach and is deployed to transform leaders, managers, team, and the entire organization from good to great and enhances organizational performance by strengthening its essential competitive advantages: Its people.

Lastly, during the last two decades the leaders in business have started realizing that organizations are not like a machine or system or process but are a collection of individuals and human beings with dreams, aspirations, and expectations. Thus, if we want to fulfill our dreams, aspirations, and create a better life for ourselves in the corporate world, then corporate coaching is the right answer to it. Because of the above factors, corporate coaching has become one of the emerging areas for human resource development function in Corporate India. Corporate coaching makes highly effective people more effective by polishing their existing rough edges. Corporate coaching adapts to employees' needs in the corporation and because corporate executives are in the different stages of their career and in varied settings, corporate coaching represents a continuum of roles, which help them learn, grow, and change.

References

Grant, A.M. (2001). *Towards a psychology of coaching*. Sydney: Coaching Psychology, University of Sydney.

Skiffington, S. & Zeus, P. (2003). *Behavioral coaching: How to build sustainable personal and organizational strength*. New Delhi: Tata McGraw-Hill.

Witherspoon, R. & White, R.P. (1997). *Four essential ways that coaching can help executives*. Greensboro, North Carolina: Centre for Creative Leadership.

CHAPTER 2

Executive Coaching

How It Works

Executive V was doing his own business for the last 15 years, and then joined an organization as Vice President-Product Support, which was a new assignment to him and he is feeling tough to handle these responsibilities. His major challenge was how to effectively handle his large team. Since he was too overworked in his professional life, his personal life was getting disturbed. He therefore came to coaching for getting help on how to delegate some of his responsibilities and improve his managerial abilities.

Executive A was heading the spare parts division of an earth-moving equipment service station. He was facing big challenges in achieving business targets and was getting stuck in taking decisions at the operational level, which resulted in loss of business.

Executive K was working as Director with an exhibition design and fabricator company, and was looking after marketing and operation of the domestic sector. His challenge was that he was not able to effectively exploit the large market where opportunities existed. He was looking for help in strategizing market penetration, business planning, and support during the implementation stage. His other challenges were to exploit the full potential of existing team members, time management, and executive presence.

Executive C was expat manager in India of a machine tool marketing company. Besides intercultural issues that he was facing, he was looking for coaching help in how to solve daily operational issues, manage his boss, and create a happy work environment.

Executive S was working at the middle level of management in a logistic company. He was facing problem in influencing others including

Contd.

Contd.

seniors in solving work-related problems, besides controlling anger at workplace and maintaining his work-life balance. He also felt a need for better work planning since he was always under pressure to meet deadlines.

Executive M was working in the telecom sector in the customer process department. He wanted to improve his ability to effectively manage his team besides enhancing his impacting and influencing skills. His self-confidence was low and he wanted to significantly improve his team's engagement score.

Executive S was heading the Sales department of an automobile agency. He was under tremendous stress in achieving business target in a highly competitive business scenario, which resulted in him losing patience. He was also short tempered and thus his personal life was getting affected.

These are some of the examples of coaching challenges the executive coaches encounter in corporations, whether large or small. However, this is not a comprehensive list of coaching issues for executive coaches, but you might have faced similar challenges at your workplace, whether you are a coach or an executive in corporation.

Before proceeding further, let us understand "what is executive coaching?" Webster dictionary defines executive as "a person who has administrative authority over an organization or division of an organization; a manager, supervisor or administrator at a high level within an organization." Based on this definition, this chapter deals with the executive coaching intervention, which is restricted not only for senior executives within an organization but also for all other executives having administrative authority, which includes senior managers, middle managers, departmental or sectional heads as well as team leaders within any organization.

In this book, we define executive coaching as

a helping relationship formed between an executive, who has managerial authority and responsibility in an organization, and an external coach, who uses a wide variety of coaching skills and techniques, to help the executive to achieve a mutually identified set of goals to improve his or her professional

performance and consequently contributing to the growth of the organization within a formally defined coaching agreement.

The ultimate goal of executive coaching is to effect sustained
change in an executive's behavior that impacts performance. The
bottom line in any coaching engagement is change. The "change"
may be in a person's actions, habits, or competencies. It may be
in their dreams and aspirations. It may be in the way they feel in
certain situations or about certain people. It may be change in how
they look at events at work or in life. Executive coaches typically
work with executives who are willing to make a sincere effort to
change and those who believe that this change will help them be
more effective at their workplace.

Executives who are most receptive to coaching are usually in
some type of transition within the organization. If people are in
certain degrees of pain, then coaching can be quite helpful because
it makes them more open to relief, learning, and reflection. The
greater the stakes and the pain, the higher the motivation for achieving successful change (Cogner, 2005). Executive coaching is effective for those executives who would say, "I want to reach there but
not sure how to reach there" (Goldsmith, 2005).

One of the biggest challenges many executives in organization
face is level of confidence, such as confidence to decide, confidence
to challenge, confidence to change, confidence to take risk, etc.
However, it is a normal and expected reaction of not knowing
something. All of us in our life faced a lack of self-confidence in
some situations. But smart executives put themselves in learning
situations to gain self-confidence to face issues and challenges in life.
The executive coach would like to help those executives who are
fighting for gaining self-confidence rather than avoiding or fleeing
for actions that could result in more confidence. Similar is the case
of fear and self-doubt. Again fear is normal and natural.

Many executives are afraid to make a decision for a variety
of reasons, such as what others will think, will I get blamed, if it
does not work, etc. The journey of executive coaching is not for
exploring why the executive is facing lack of confidence or having

self-doubt, but creating opportunities so that the executives develop confidence to move ahead.

Any executive coaching intervention in an organization goes through the following broad steps:

- Pre-coaching
- Contracting
- Assessment
- Coaching agenda setting
- Coaching process
- Closure

This chapter covers each step of the executive coaching intervention, so that whether you are a sponsor of the executive coaching intervention in your organization or you are the executive identified for coaching or the reporting officer of the executive undergoing coaching or you are the executive coach, you will get clarity what are your roles vis-à-vis others in the executive coaching program.

Pre-Coaching

The responsibility of the sponsor, which is normally HR in the organization or someone at the senior level of management nominated by the organization, is to identify coaches, select right coaches for the organization, set up contracts with the coaches, ensure that the coaches understand the organizational context, explain the role of the management and the expectations of management from the coaching intervention. The sponsor also explains to the coaches the purpose, objectives, processes, and expected outcomes from the executive coaching intervention. It is almost important for the organization to identify the executives, who have a genuine need for executive coaching and are willing as well as ready to go through the coaching program.

For setting up an executive coaching program, the following tasks are to be undertaken:

1. To create a pool of executive coaches
2. To identify the executives who need coaching
3. To match the coach and the executive according to coaching needs, compatibility, and chemistry
4. To ensure that there is a clear purpose established and communicated to all stakeholders

To create a pool of executive coaches, every organization follows its own process. The most common approaches are contacting the coaching service provider firm or contacting the executive coaches directly. In the first approach, the organization contacts one or two firms who have a pool of approved executive coaches. The organization then selects the coaches from the pool based on the coaching credential, professional experience, and academic background. In the second approach, the organization contacts the coaches directly from the available databank or the coaches listed at various coaching forums, viz., International Coaching Federation, Association of Coaching, etc.

The second important aspect of pre-coaching step is the identification of executives who will be undergoing coaching and preparing them. The organization articulates adequately within the organization why executive coaching interventions are being undertaken and what are the long-term expectations of the management. Each executive, who has been identified for coaching, would definitely like to know why he has been selected and what are the expectations of the management from him. It is also important for the management to communicate to the peers of these selected executives as to why they are not in the part of the interventions, the objectives of the intervention as well as the selection criteria of the executive for the intervention.

The next action is to decide which coach will get associated with which executive(s). Whatever the experiences and background of coaches may be, each executive coach brings different competencies, styles, and approaches on the table. Normally, organizations either arrange a brief meeting between the executive and the executive coaches (two to three) or each executive is provided with details of two to three coaches, so that they can choose one coach for themselves.

The executive coaches and the sponsor then finalize logistics issues of scheduling sessions, duration of session, mode of delivery, whether it would be face to face and/or telephonic, session cancellation protocols, what to expect or what not to expect from the coaching process, etc.

Contracting

After identifying the coaches to be engaged in the organization, the next step for the sponsor is to decide with the coach what to do, which is called contracting. The basic premise of contracting in executive coaching is to clarify goals and processes so that there are productive outcomes at the end of the coaching journey and there is no misunderstanding amongst all the stockholders, i.e., the coach, the sponsor, and the executive.

There are mainly three components in contracting:

- Clarifying the goals for coaching
- Explaining the coaching process
- Finalizing the broad coaching agenda, terms, deliverables, organizational support, the role of the sponsor, etc.

Annexure 2.1 gives an example of a coaching engagement process outline of an executive coaching program of an organization.

The initial meeting between the coach and the sponsor is aimed at clarifying the sponsor's goals and expectations from the coaching intervention for the executive, who will be undergoing the coaching. It is also important to include other key influencers, viz., reporting officer, departmental or functional head, head of learning and development besides HR from the sponsor side, in the interaction.

From this interaction, the coach collects data of current performance level of the executive from multiple sources and also the future developmental need of the executive. Since each coach follows his/her unique process of coaching, it is important for the sponsor to check that there is an alignment between the processes the coach will typically follow with the defined or intended coaching process of the organization. If there is a difference, then it is important to check whether it is acceptable to the organization or not. The coach generally explains how he will engage with the executives, what are the assessments tools that will be used, what data supports are required from the organization, how the action plan will be made, at which stages the sponsor will be briefed on the progress made, and how and when the coaching effectiveness will be evaluated.

Finally, the coach and the sponsor jointly finalize the coaching contract, which includes the following:

- Objectives of coaching engagement
- Timeline
- Coaching fee
- Number of coaching sessions and duration of each coaching session
- Expected outcomes
- Role of sponsors
- Confidentiality agreement
- Termination of coaching engagement

The coach then meets with the executive to understand the context of the executive, i.e., his background, his role, what are his current challenges, what are his key result areas, how he perceives his role in the organization, what are his expectations from coaching, etc. The basic purpose of this meeting is to see if there is chemistry between the coach and the executive. The coach, on the other hand, explains to the executive as to what is coaching all about, what is his role as a coach, what he expects from the executive during the engagement, the detailed coaching process, the scope and objectives of the engagement, and how the coaching results will be evaluated. The coach also answers to all the questions, apprehensions, or doubts the executive may have. This is an opportunity for both the coach and the executive to make personal assessment about each other. The coach may explore in this meeting the following questions:

Am I the right coach for this executive?

Is the executive open, ready, reflective, curious, and motivated?

Annexure 2.2 gives an example of some of the ground rules of coaching expectations.

Assessment

The purpose of the assessment is to collect relevant data of the executive, based on which the coaching agenda and detailed development plan are to be developed. In other words, the assessment phase of executive coaching is to understand where the executive is at present. The assessment process varies widely depending on the type of organization as well as the coaching objectives.

Before starting the assessment, the executive coach collects information about the executive, e.g., his education and professional backgrounds, job responsibilities and role, who are his team members, whom he reports to, who are his reportees, etc. This information is generally available with the human resource department of the organization. The coach then meets with the executive to understand from him what are his dreams and aspirations, what are the important events that have taken place in his life so far, how he perceives his role in the organization, what are his work challenges, etc.

The next stage is conducting assessment. Executive coaches generally conduct a formal 360-degree assessment or 360-degree interview with key stakeholders of the executive concerned. While conducting the 360-degree assessment, it is important for the coach to identify executives to be contacted for getting feedback about this individual, the dimensions of assessment as well the process of collecting information. It is preferred that the coachee (executive) is also involved besides the sponsor of the program (generally human resource department) in selecting the persons from whom the feedback will be collected. This helps the executive not only accept feedback with a more open mind at a later stage but also bring a sense of involvement from the executive from the beginning itself. Some coaches ask the executive to contact potential interviewees for requesting their participation, whereas other coaches contact the potential interviewees either directly or through Human Resources, and inform them that the executive has mentioned their name as potential interviewee. Though each coach will have a different set of dimensions of assessment, the dimensions covered in 360-degree assessment (or interview) are to identify what are the executive's strengths and developmental needs in key managerial competencies like interpersonal skills, making decision, team handling ability, planning, managing performances, workplace behavior, work-related skills, etc.

It is also essential that all the assessment data or one-to one interview data are kept anonymous and the summary of assessment is prepared and shared with the executive. Some organizations conduct 360-degree assessment periodically. In that case, the coach may not conduct additional 360-degree assessment, provided the last assessment was conducted not later than six months earlier.

The coach may also use various personality, behavioral, managerial, leadership styles, or work preferences, inventories (details of such instruments are given in Chapter 8), etc. The coach also looks into performance appraisal data of the executive, mainly appraiser assessment of performance of the appraisee on the areas of improvements, talent or succession planning data, employee engagement score, assessment centre data, etc., if available. The aim of this process is to get multiple perspectives of the executive from different sources in the organization. Some executive coaches prefer to conduct direct observations of the executive at the workplace for one to two days, i.e., shadow coaching.

Coaching Agenda Setting

By now, the coach has a complete understanding of the executive's strengths, areas requiring attention, the dreams and aspirations of the executives, the challenges the executive is facing as well as blind spots of the executive. However, the coaching agenda is to be set by the coachee and not by the coach. As the proverb goes, "you can take the horse to river but cannot force him to drink water." If the horse is thirsty, then only he will drink water. Similar is the case in coaching. If the executive would like to improve certain areas of his life, whether personal or work life, and needs support of the coach, then the coaching journey will be effective.

The coach presents his feedback/observations based on the data received from multiple perspectives to the executive. Normally, executive coaches make summary notes of his observations along with some evidence, while making his observations absolutely anonymous and objective as far as possible. As the coach and the executive discuss the feedback, the coach keeps in mind that whatever data he has gathered and collated is not necessarily universal truth but collections of perceptions based on displayed behavior and actions of the executive. The purpose of the feedback session is for the executive to understand the messages from the feedback, to make a sense out of it and reflect upon. Hence, the basic objectives of sharing the feedback to the executive are as follows:

1. To identify issues emerging from the collective feedback
2. To identify the issues where the executive agrees with
3. To identify issues where the executive disagrees with
4. To identify issues where the executive needs more information or clarification or is not sure what it meant to him
5. To check if there is a pattern
6. To see if there is any surprise for the executive

The coach will ask the executive to reflect on the feedback and to draw his/her own conclusions. The coach allows the executive to reflect on these observations and ask the executive what are his perspectives on areas the executive feels relevant and important for his self-growth and improvement of his effectiveness at the workplace from both short-term and long-term perspectives. The feedback from the coach gives an opportunity to the executive to have a clear picture of who he is now and what he wants to be in the future. The executive may be asked open-ended questions about his perceptions of his own strengths and developmental needs, and encourages him to rank his developmental needs in order of priority. It is a good idea if the coach gives a task to the executive to list out what are his strength areas, what are his developmental needs, and what are the areas he thinks he needs to change for betterment.

Coaching Process

People come to coaching for different reasons but ultimately they are looking for change, whether to have more or less of something, from both personal and work life. Therefore, whether it is executive coaching or life coaching or any other niche areas of coaching, the bottom line is change. Coaching process is often like peeling layers on an onion. The initial phase is peeling a few layers, one by one, then as the process goes deeper, the process passes through peeling more and more layers together.

Coaches typically follow their own coaching process, based on their own style of coaching as well as the coaching agenda of the executive. "Models" or visual representations are used by the coaches to illustrate what is done in a particular process. Having a model, along with a written description of a process, supports the coach to articulate what they will do. It also gives the executive a visual framework to understand what the coaching process will look like. By having a clearly defined model, the coach has an easier time explaining to the executive what will take place during the coaching sessions. Through a coaching model, the coach synthesizes tools, techniques, and frameworks from a range of approaches in helping people initiate and sustain a journey on the goal-directed personal change. Hence it is important to understand the change process so that coaches can navigate with coachees in the change journey in a step-by-step process.

The Delta Coaching Model as seen in Figure 2.1 is a visual representation of a change that happens as the executive undertakes the coaching journey with the support of his or her coach. The Delta or triangle shape in mathematics represents an increment or variation. In coaching, the coach is always looking for how the coachee could move forward in his or her life journey, and how the coach can facilitate the process to help that happen. The triangle or delta symbol represents the total coaching process in two different ways: (1) each component or segment is an integral part of the coaching process and (2) each component or segment builds on the components or segments below them. In other words, without a proper base or foundation and strong support structures, the ultimate success of the coaching journey, i.e., the peak of the Delta, is far from reachable and likely unsustainable. The coach maintains a focus on the coachee, the coaching process as a whole, and the coachee's context, and in response to what he or she observes in relation to any or all of these elements the coach selects a way of working with the coachee that seems appropriate and likely to be effective. The coaches can navigate with coachees in the change journey in a step-by-step process, as depicted in the Delta Coaching model. Let us now discuss each segment of the model in the context of the coaching process.

CREATE
RELATIONSHIP

During the coaching journey, the coach first creates a relationship with the coachee. Relationship is the foundation of any coaching journey. As it is in any building structure, if the foundation is not properly constructed, the building cannot stand for long.

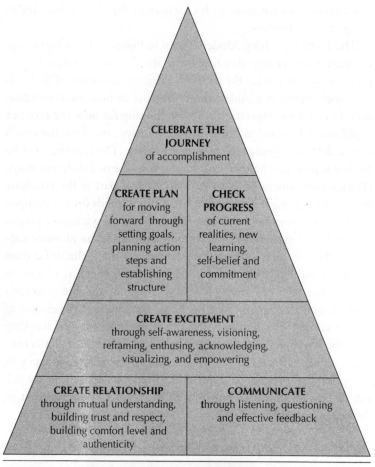

Figure 2.1 Delta Coaching Model of Change

The Leaning Tower of Pisa in Italy is one such example of unstable foundation. Hence, the coach takes utmost care in building a relationship with the executive. The coaching relationship is built based on commitment, mutual trust, and respect.

The coaching relationship is not just chemistry between the coach and the executive but much more delicate and sensitive. In executive coaching scenario, the coach is brought inside the organization by Human Resource department and the coachee is selected mostly by the organization. There is always in the mind of the executive that the coach is more accountable to the sponsor of the intervention for meeting their expectations than that of the executive. Therefore, the coach makes extra effort to ensure that the executive understands that though the coach is hired by the organization, the commitment of the coach is toward the development of the executive, which in turn impacts the organization. Just saying this to the executive does not suffice. The executive needs to feel and be convinced that his coach is keen for his development and there is sincere commitment from the coach for his growth and development.

The second important aspect of relationship is mutual trust. If there is no mutual trust between the coach and the executive, there is no coaching relationship. Trust is a delicate flower, it can flourish only when the coach can create the right environment by displaying a high level of integrity, honesty, openness, fairness, and respect. Sometimes, the coach inadvertently breaks his commitment to the executive. For example, the coach promises the executive to send an email or to call on a particular day or to get some material in the next session, but forget to do so. The message goes to the executive that he is not important. Many times, the executive notices that the coach does not "walk the talk," viz., the coach expects the executive to be on time for the session but the coach reaches late for session for one or other reasons.

When the coach creates an atmosphere of trust and makes the executive feel valued and competent, this in turn leads to self-motivation of the executive. One simple principle I follow in every coaching engagement is I never discussed anything about the executive and/or about the coaching journey of the executive with any member of the organization, including his reporting officer and the sponsor of the assignment, if the executive is not present in the meeting. The exception is only during 360-degree assessment.

Similarly, respect is more a feeling than just mere words. The executives feel respected when they are accepted as they are, not as they ought to be. Sometimes, the coach breaks the confidentiality agreement and shares some of the issues discussed in the coaching session with other members of the organization, which the executive comes to know, then whatever trust developed painstakingly will be destroyed immediately. Trust also comes from being authentic. For example, I always openly share my own experiences, fears, passions, successes, and failures with all of my coachees.

Transparency between the executive and the coach also contributes in building relationship. The executive needs to be clear in his mind that there is no hidden agenda from the coach's side or the coach is not manipulating him to achieve the agenda of the coaching. The more the coach gives opportunity to the executive to discuss whatever issues the executive wishes to bring into coaching, the more the executive feels comfortable with the coach. The executive coach creates a safe space in which the executives can feel comfortable to reflect, share, and take risk in developing themselves.

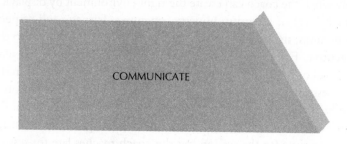

COMMUNICATE

After establishing trust and intimacy with the coachee, the coach needs to connect with the executive at the emotional level. A good communication starts with active listening. A major part of any communication goes beyond the spoken words; hence, the coach requires to pick up the message, intent, and feelings from the coaching conversation. The executive needs to feel secure and comfortable when he is discussing his personal issues with the coach.

Coaching conversation focuses on creating awareness within the executive of the present state and its implication as well as reflecting on the way forward. In the coaching conversation, both the coach and the executive think deeply each issue together. The coach uses tools such as questioning, listening, probing, mirroring, and framing perspectives so that the executive can get deeper insights.

CHECK PROGRESS

After creating a proper foundation of the coaching journey, the role of the coach is to create excitement within the executive. The coach assists the executives to visualize successes and asks them to explore the consequences of not taking actions. The visualization exercise could be asking the executive to imagine the situation, where he has already reached, then think and feel how he will behave or act in that situation. Many executives have limited capacity to look beyond, where they need support from the coach. Sometimes, fear of taking actions, risk of negative outcomes, past failure, or disappointments create a self-limiting belief in the mind of the executive. In that situation, the coach enthuses the executive by appreciating their inner talent, the journey the executive has taken so far, and their ability to take actions in the past. Sometimes, the coach also shares some similar success stories with the executive to create confidence in the mind of the executive. Excitement starts happening in the mind of the executive when the executive understands clearly what are the current realities, where he would like to reach as well as how compelling is the destination. The coach presents perspectives from higher levels than where the executive is now at present. The role of the coach is just to frame perspectives and present a vision for the executive but not to suggest or define the end-state for the executive. Taking the example from the famous epic of Hindu mythology, Mahabharata, Krishna showed Arjuna the consequences of going for the war, but Arjuna was to decide whether he would like to go for war or not.

Self-determination theory (Ryan and Deci, 2000) claims that when the following three human needs are satisfied, people are intrinsically motivated, able to fulfill their potentialities, and able to seek out progressively greater challenges:

- *Autonomy:* the need to choose what one is doing, being an agent of one's life

- *Competence:* the need to feel confident in doing what one is doing

- *Relatedness:* the need to have human connections that are close and secure, while still respecting autonomy and facilitating competence

In the coaching scenario, the coach ensures the executive's autonomy by allowing them to make their own decisions. The coach also supports the executive to enhance their competence by discussing with them their strengths, inner talents as well as their past accomplishments. The coach also sometimes discusses how their strengths could be useful in the present situation and also gives examples of similar situations, where other people like him have succeeded in similar situations. Relatedness needs of the executive are addressed by the coach by encouraging, enthusing, and acknowledging the executive all through the coaching process by empathic listening, establishing trust, openness, and mutual understanding.

Sharp (2011) proposes some examples of how one can create and enhance positivity in the early stages of coaching with a view to increase the chances of coachee's (executive) achievement:

- Actively and explicitly focus on positive experiences within the coachee's life, present and past.

- Quickly work toward helping the coachee identify his or her strengths, specially looking for expressions of these strengths in past experiences and discuss how best to utilize these in future situations.

- Cultivate hope and optimism at every opportunity by reminding the coachee of previous successes and achievements and by appropriately noting how these experiences can be used to build more positivity in the future.

- Make the coachees feel special and do what you can to make them believe that the process of coaching is and will be a positive one.

Let us look into one such case...

Coachee C was born in Madrid but went to live in Venezuela with her mother. She was married twice and divorced. After her second divorce, she started her own furniture rental business alone in Spain with "no money." After 18 years, having owned a showroom in Madrid and Barcelona and 23 coachee/employees, she sold the business and migrated to the United States. In the United States, she started working as a personal assistant to a large real estate property owner, helping her boss in managing her business.

During the coaching conversation, it emerged that she would like to plan an alternate future in Spain. She was not sure about her future goals and she was expressing a sense of despair and helplessness during coaching session. During subsequent sessions, the focus of coaching shifted to a value-based goal-setting process. One of her goals was to go back to Spain and start a small venture. During the process of identifying possible roadblocks and resources required to achieve the goal, she was not feeling confident about herself in achieving this challenging goal and it was noticed that her self-efficacy was very low.

The next stage in coaching (discovery) was focused on her self-efficacy. The coach helped her look back on her accomplishments to date. Initially, she could not list even three major accomplishments. To assist her in the reflection process, the coach shared with her what the coach had observed to be some of her major accomplishments, such as starting a furniture rental business from nothing to having two showrooms now, settling in the United States at the age of 54, and bringing up three children as a single parent. With this feedback, she realized her strengths and started feeling confident about herself.

To continue this process, it was decided that she would ask ten acquaintances to relate good and positive aspects about her, which they had observed. She was successful in getting eight responses out of which four observations surprised her because she was not aware of those personal qualities that they had noticed. She shared in the subsequent session how this process had helped her see herself in a different perspective and how she had started feeling confident about herself.

The coaching conversation aims to create a picture of the end state so that the executive can focus on the right target. The executive starts exploring how the success of his coaching journey will look like, to clearly see and define the goal post, and to explore alternate paths to reach the end state. The coach assists the executive to develop self-awareness and to look into the bigger picture so that the executive could see clearly where he would like to reach. Sometimes, it is difficult for the executive to visualize the goal post. The executive may not see the complete picture, what is possible, and what needs to happen.

The next coaching session is devoted on broad agenda setting. The executive with the support of the coach will identify one or two major areas where the executive feels the need for change for six to nine months. It could be on a particular behavior that he would like to change, develop, or improve or one or more managerial competencies he would like to develop or learn a new skill or working on specific performance issues or achieving specific business results.

In some situations, the executive may not be clear of what they want in their life, why they want something in life, and how they are going to achieve their goals, whether professional, work-related, or personal goals. The reason could be the executives are not aware of their values, since it remains hidden in the recesses of their subconscious. In other words, they are not clear of what they want in their life, why they want something in life, and how they are going to get their goals. Even in some situations, the executives may be clear about their goals and how to achieve these goals, there is a lack of commitment to follow the path of achieving their goals. This happens when goals are not based on the values of the executive. Values are like a beacon for an individual. One needs to keep their values in view in order to remain focused and be in the right direction. The executive coach assists the executive to get them clarity on what are their values first before going for goal setting. Values play an important role in the executives' life, since their values inspire them for action, direct their lives, and influence the decision they take. When the goals are developed that match with the executive's interest and that are congruent with the executive's core values, the executive is generally more positively oriented in taking actions.

According to cognitive dissonance theory (Festinger, 1957), there is a tendency for an individual to seek consistency with their cognition. In value-based goal setting process, cognitive dissonance may surface in the coaching process if there is a misalignment of individual values with the goals the executive would like to achieve or when more than one contrasting but attractive or compelling perspective emerges (Mukherjee, 2008). An important consequence of the theory of cognitive dissonance is that people are motivated to work at a level consistent with their self-perceptions of competency toward the task they are undertaking. Bandura (1994) quotes that self-efficacy beliefs determine how people feel, think, motivate themselves, and behave. A strong sense of efficacy enhances human accomplishment and personal well-being in many ways. People with high assurance in their capabilities approach difficult tasks as challenges to be mastered rather than as threats to be avoided. In contrast, people who doubt their capabilities shy away from difficult tasks, which they view as personal threats. They have low aspirations and weak commitments to the goals they choose to pursue. Dissonance is the most powerful when it is about self-image. When the coach encourages a feeling of competency in task areas as well as general feelings of competency in the mind of the executive, the motivation to work toward the goal, in general, is increased. Executives can be helped to develop a belief that they can make a change. In that situation, the coach encourages the executives to reflect on the major changes they have already undergone in life, thereby creating an awareness of their inherent skills or talents Another approach the coach uses is to enhance the self-efficacy of executives by improving their perception of self-competency using strengths inventory assessment process or asking them to remember situations when they had successfully accomplished similar tasks.

After defining the end state, the executive starts exploring various options and alternatives to reach the goal. Typically the coaching conversation in this phase is to brainstorm with the executive to identify as many as possible alternative actions to achieve the target. For example, if the executive is working on coming to office on time. So far what he is doing is not working for him. The purpose of brainstorming with the executive is to identify what he could do differently so that he will arrive in office on time. The executive may identify some of the following possible options:

1. To start early from home
2. To get up early in the morning
3. To go to sleep early
4. To change the mode of transport
5. To come along with another office colleague
6. To ask wife to make him leave home on time
7. To have a detailed plan for every morning
8. To shift his home near office
9. To make temporary arrangement to stay near office during weekdays
10. To skip one or two morning chores
11. To own vehicle
12. To come with office transport
13. To reach home on time
14. To avoid late-night engagement

After identifying all options, it may emerge that some options may not be feasible for the executive. That is absolutely ok. After identifying all possible options through brainstorming, the executive then evaluates each option one by one and shortlists two or three options which the executive may feel feasible, effective, and doable. The coach assists the executive to evaluate each alternative one by one based on the feasibility and effectiveness of the alternative in achieving results. Sometimes, the coach gives his perspectives during evaluation of each option. After identifying the options, the executive also identifies obstacles, roadblocks, and challenges in front of him. If all the obstacles are not identified, the actions required to overcome the hurdles could not be identified. After identifying the best options, the coach encourages the executive to decide a detailed action plan with specific timelines. While developing action item, the coach assists the executive to identify what are the supports required from others, what resources he needs, and what are the milestones. It is also important to check the commitment level of the executive of taking action in this stage by checking with the executive that all agreed actions will be acted upon. This is important since it is natural for people to get lazy after initiating the process. Each big action needs to be broken into many small actions or baby steps with specific timelines, so that the executive is clear of every step of the journey.

CHECK PROGRESS

Coaching is largely a change process that leads toward a predetermined destination of goal achievement. The coach's job is to facilitate the executive through the coaching process to support the executive moving into action to achieve his or her goals. The coach creates a structure with the executive of a follow-up plan and check-in opportunities. The role of the coach is to make the executives excited about the first action they are going to take and assuring them the coach will support them throughout the process. The executive needs continuous acknowledgment from the coach while taking actions and the coach lets the executive know that there is approval from the coach whatever actions the executive takes.

Each coaching session starts with the review of progress of the action plan, what could be achieved or not achieved, what actions are completed or not completed, the exploration of what could be done in moving forward, and fine-tune the action plan, milestones, and targets as appropriate. The coaching conversation focuses on:

- Reviewing what happened, both planned and unplanned
- Reviewing what could not happen
- Reviewing obstacles faced, challenges encountered, what actions didn't work
- Reexamining current realities, the commitments, and interest level of the executives
- Reviewing goals, actions, and targets
- Discussing the way forward

Though it sometimes looks mundane, in my own experience in coaching I observed that some of my very senior successful executive coaching clients are very good in planning and follow-up for others but when it involves them in person, they falter. Executives may commit that it is their journey, they have accepted themselves to take actions, but if there is no strong accountability partnership from the coach, the executive may not take all actions as planned. The reasons could be many. Hence, the coach builds the robust review mechanism in the planning stage so that both the executive and the coach have clarity of the process. In fact, most of my coaching executives appreciated the rigor at later stage, though they had some reluctance in the beginning for regular reviews. The coach continuously acknowledges the executive on the actions the executive has taken and done something, whether successful or unsuccessful during the review conversation. The role of the coach is as cheerleader and supporter, so that the executive feels good and encouraged.

CELEBRATE
THE
JOURNEY

One of the most important roles for the coach is to acknowledge, enthuse, and recognize the executive of their achievement, whenever it occurs. The executive may not be celebrating his accomplishment but the coach creates opportunity to celebrate achievements/small win for the executive and encourages the executive to enjoy the success and share his accomplishment with others. Many executives are not in the habit of celebrating or comfortable in sharing success with others. The more senior the executive, the less they celebrate their accomplishment; even many of them feel uncomfortable to share their successes with their friends, peers, and close family members. In coaching, it is not only the journey that is important, but also enjoying the arrival of the and destination of the journey. It is worth celebrating the small steps of successes in the coaching journey as the executive moves to reach the major goals in life and workplace. While executives celebrate their successes, whether small or big, it provides the opportunity for other stockholders to participate in the accomplishment and allows the executive to acknowledge them for what they have contributed for the success of the executive. As a coach, I always insist that my executive coaching clients share gratitude with those who helped them directly or indirectly, take the family for outing or dinner, pray to God, indulge themselves on something they love to do or what they have not done for a long time, or buy something special, since celebration means different for every individual.

Closure

The closure phase of a coaching engagement happens when the coaching process is ended with the executive. The sponsor would like to assess the coaching process, the benefits achieved by the executive, and also to make decision about the executive coach and future use of coaching interventions in the organization. The measurement of impact of the coaching engagement is an important part in this phase. Many organizations conduct dip-stick surveys with key stakeholders after the end of the coaching journey to assess the progress of the coaching. Some organizations conduct reviewing meetings among sponsor of the program, reporting officer of the executive, the executive, and the coach at the mid of the coaching process. During this meeting, the coaching agenda and the coaching goals are reviewed. The other stakeholders in turn give their perspectives on the changes they have observed or encountered in the skills, performance, or behavior of the executive.

The next step of the closure phase is transitioning into a long-term development journey. After completing the coaching engagement, the organization sponsor plans whatever actions are necessary to ensure that the executive will be able to continue his developmental journey as well as whatever gains were by the coaching does not get lost over a period of time. The executive coach, the reporting officer of the executive, sponsor of the engagement, and the executive jointly formulate the long-term development plan based on identified specific areas of focus, which include the areas where gaps exists or further work is needed. This meeting will also deliberate the future action plan, identify the process owner and the reviewing mechanism.

Chapter Summary

As defined earlier, executive coaching is an experiential and individualized leadership development process to build leaders' capacity to achieve short- and long-term organizational goals. It is done through one-to-one interactions. It is grounded in data from multiple perspectives and based on mutual trust and respect. Executive coaching typically works with executives who are willing to make a sincere effort to change.

Executive coaching in organizations goes through broad steps such as pre-coaching activities, contracting, assessment, coaching agenda setting, coaching process, and closure.

Pre-coaching is the phase where the sponsors identify and select the right coaches, identify executives with genuine need for coaching, and is ready to go through the coaching process. At this stage sponsors ideally and necessarily with the involvement of the executive decide which coach will get associated with which executive. Executives are briefed about the objectives, methodology, and methods of delivery of the coaching process.

In the contracting phase, the coach and sponsor jointly finalize the coaching contract outlining the coaching agreement, timeline, coaching fee, number of coaching sessions, expected outcomes, etc. The coach then meets with the executive to gain clarity of his and organization's needs and priorities. This interaction also helps the coach and the executive to build chemistry for working together.

During assessment phase, the coach with the help of executive and his stakeholders in the organization understands the executive's strengths, areas of improvement, and leadership style. Coach may make use of different techniques such as 360-degree assessment, interview, performance appraisal report, etc. to gather information. The coach tries to get multiple perspectives about the executive.

It is the executive with the help of the coach who sets the agenda. The coach presents the feedback gathered in the course of assessment and encourages the executive to reflect on them. Executive with assistance from coach identifies one or two major areas for development to enhance his effectiveness. The next step would be to develop a detailed action plan to achieve the goal.

Coaching process is like peeling layers and go deeper. The coach enables the executive to navigate the change journey in a step-by-step process. It is also important in building a coaching relationship with the executive based on commitment, mutual trust, and respect. Coach needs to demonstrate this by action and behavior to get the executive's confidence and thereby build a coaching relationship.

After establishing trust and intimacy with the executive, the coach needs to connect with the executive at an emotional level. This happens with active listening. Coach needs to pick up the message, intent, and feelings from the coaching conversation. The executive needs to feel secured and comfortable. After creating a proper foundation of the coaching journey, the coach needs to build excitement in the executive. The coach assists the executive to develop goals in line with the executive's interest and in congruence with core values so that the executive is more positively oriented in taking action for change. The coach encourages the executive to decide a detailed action plan with a timeline. Executive at times may falter to implement the action plan if there is no strong accountability partnership from the coach. Hence the coach builds a strong review mechanism.

The role of the coach is also that of a cheerleader and supporter, so that the executive feels good and encouraged. Coach encourages the executive to celebrate achievements small or big.

The closure phase of coaching engagement happens when the coaching process is ended with the executive. During this phase coaching goals are reviewed. The next step of the closure phase is transitioning into long-term development.

Annexure 2.1: A Sample Coaching Engagement Process Outline

Intention

Company M's coaching program provides accelerated personal development for engineers in demanding customer-facing roles. It has been designed to deliver the developmental priorities of each engineer in an accelerated learning environment. Through shadowing, the coach is able to witness the engineers' performance in a real-time environment and to customize the development effort as appropriate. Highly integrated with the engineers' regular workday, it will minimize the need to take time out for personal development.

Program Summary

Each engineer will spend two days with an expert coach over a three months period. This will include experiential coaching at the customer site, personal coaching at Company M, and development planning with their manager. The developmental agenda will be set by the line manager and contracted with the engineer. All coaches bring a deep knowledge of the developmental challenges of technical customer-facing roles combined with an expert understanding of coaching for accelerated performance.

Program elements

Matching process	HR manager contacts Org X to discuss an engineer joining the coaching program. This conversation is typically 10–15 minutes long and will review development goals and the potential fit of the coaching program.	Development briefing
	Based on this, Org X will select the best coach for the assignment and brief this coach on the developmental objectives.	Coach matching
	The assigned coach will organize a 10–15-minutes phone call where coach and engineer can introduce each other and check for compatibility.	

Coaching intake	Engineer will complete coaching intake questions and (optional) submit previous performance and development plans. Coaching guide provides on how to get the best out of the coaching.	Coaching intake questions
		Coaching guide
	This will ensure a common understanding of the coaching approach and ensure that the coach is briefed on the broader background of the engineer.	
	A three-way meeting between the coach, engineer, and line manager to introduce development goals from line manager, integrate engineer's perspective, and develop a clear plan for the coaching.	Three-way contracting
		Coaching outcomes plan
Shadow coaching	Four half-day coaching sessions with the engineer.	
	The majority of these sessions will be organized around "live" situations including team meetings, presentations, issue management, executive meetings, and workshops. Coaching will generally take place before and after these live situations.	
	At other times, the coach will be in observer mode, studying performance and identifying opportunities for change that can be integrated into the coaching time.	
	There is also provision for some coaching sessions to take place at Company M's office where the development objectives make this preferable.	
	Following the coaching session, the engineer will complete a session recap process to identify key learning and provide input to the coaching process.	Coaching recap process
Integration	A three-way meeting between the coach, engineer, and line manager to review progress against development goals and experience of the coaching work.	Three-way review
	Engineer completes feedback form on the coaching and the line manager forwards this to Org X with their own comments added.	Feedback

Annexure 2.2: A Sample of Coaching Expectations Sheet

What You Can Expect from Me

I believe that you are capable and resourceful and that you have your own answers, even if you are not immediately aware of them or confident in your ability to access them. My job is to listen with an open heart, ask provocative questions, and offer tools, structures, ideas, inquiries, requests, and activities that will help you tap into your inner source of wisdom.

1. I will always assume that you are doing your best.
2. I will be your champion, always holding a vision of your best self for you.
3. I will ask you to stretch.
4. I will ask you to think outside the box.
5. I will ask you to have faith in Divine guidance, and to develop spiritual practices that honor your personal spiritual path.
6. I will make powerful requests. The purpose of a powerful request is to assist you in accomplishing your goals. You are free to accept, decline, or make a counter offer. If you choose to decline a request, together we will find a way that works better for you.
7. I will manage my own judgments and language rigorously.
8. I will take good care of myself so I can be my best for our work together.
9. I will continue to learn and grow through self-study, personal and professional development training, and by working with my own professional coach.
10. I will abide by our coaching agreement, by my Code of Ethics, and by the Ethical Guidelines of the International Coach Federation (www.coachfederation.com).
11. I will not take life or myself too seriously—and I will encourage you to do the same!

What I Ask of You as My Executive

1. Do your best but don't try to be perfect.
2. Communicate with me honestly and fully.
3. Be coach-able; partner with me to facilitate your process of living, learning and growing
4. Take responsibility for your results, both the successes and the failures.
5. Have a positive mental attitude.
6. Come from a place of love and kindness.
7. Have a high level of honesty and integrity; be honest about your life and your actions.
8. Be open and vulnerable. Risk showing the real you.
9. Do what you say you will do.

Annexure 2.3: A Sample Coaching Engagement Contract

1. The coach will use 360-degree assessment and EQI assessment report during coaching, which is available with you. The coach may administer additional psychometric assessment tools, such as MBTI, DISC, etc., as per requirement.
2. The coach will conduct face-to-face coaching and/or telephonic sessions for you once in a month for 120 minutes duration. All the face-to-face sessions will be at executive's place.
3. The dates will be intimated to the executive by the coach in the beginning of every month or at least 15 days before or at the end of each coaching session.
4. Coaching sessions will be fixed based on mutual consent between executive and coach and mode of coaching will be based on mutual convenience.
5. Each session (face-to-face or telephonic) will be of 120 minutes duration. There will be 6 (six) sessions in total.
6. The executives will be responsible for ensuring their availability for the sessions.
7. The coach will also conduct telephonic coaching as per the coaching agenda. Executives will call the coach for the coaching session on his Skype/Phone at the scheduled time, unless advised otherwise.
8. The coach and executive agree to provide each other with at least 24 hours notice to reschedule an appointment, except in the case of unforeseeable emergency. Both parties agree to meet promptly at the agreed time and to be available for the entire duration of the session.
9. Between sessions, executive may email the coach anytime at xxx@yyy.com or call him at XXXX. If a response has been requested, the coach will endeavor to do so within two business days (usually sooner). The only exception will be when the coach is out of town or during a holiday. However, the coach will let the executives know when he

is unavailable. Executive is expected to place a high priority on this intervention. It is important for the integrity of the process that agreed-upon schedules are kept to. The coach will try his best to accommodate minor changes in timing. In case of emergencies, the timings will be worked around. The coach will also try not to cancel appointments with the executive on a short notice for business reasons, but may do so for personal reasons such as family emergencies, though he will seek to avoid this.

a. The coaching will last for six months, depending on the coaching agenda, which may be extended on mutually agreed terms, if required.
b. Broadly 70 percent of the coaching will be face-to-face and 30 percent will be over the telephone.

A review of coaching process may be conducted in the fourth and seventh months, to assess the impact of coaching at the workplace. The executive's organization will re-administer 360-degree assessment and EQI as per the talent management program plan.

References

Bandura, A. (1994). Self-efficacy. In V.S. Ramachaudran (ed.), *Encyclopedia of human behavior*, Vol. 4, pp. 71–81. New York: Academic Press.

Cogner, J. (2005). Coaching leaders. In H. Morgan, P. Harkins, & M. Goldsmith (eds), *The art and practice of leadership coaching*. Hoboken, New Jersey: John Wiley & Sons.

Festinger, L. (1957). *A theory of cognitive dissonance*. Palo Alto, California: Stanford University Press.

Goldsmith, M. (2005). Changing leadership behavior. In H. Morgan, P. Harkins, & M. Goldsmith (eds), *The art and practice of leadership coaching*, pp. 56–60. Hoboken, New Jersey: John Wiley & Sons. Inc.

Mukherjee, S. (2008). Behavioral change process in coaching. *IJCO*, 2, pp. 87–100.

Ryan, R.M. & Deci, E.L. (2000). Self-determination theory and the facilitation of intrinsic motivation and well-being. *American Psychologist*, 55, pp. 68–78.

Sharp, T. (2011). The primacy of positivity—applications in a coaching context. *Coaching: An International Journal of Theory, Research and Practice*, 4 (1), pp. 42–49.

CHAPTER 3

Behavioral Coaching
Concept, Strategies, and Processes

Before dealing with the topic of behavioral coaching, let me briefly dwell on the word, "behavior." Behavior is basically goal oriented. The basic unit of behavior is an activity, and in fact, all behaviors are a series of activities. Any behavior is generally motivated by a desire to satisfy a need or set of needs. Motives are the "whys" of behavior. Motives are concerned with the needs that drive behavior. Motives may be conscious or subconscious. In coaching, the coach encourages the executives to identify steps to be undertaken to achieve their goals. The activities the executive undertakes to achieve the goals are the behaviors of the executive.

All of us usually have two major questions in our life: "What we desire to achieve" and "How we wish to achieve that." The answers to these two questions of "What" and "How" often result in a dilemma to decide between the two opposing forces of life. We resolve the dilemma with the aid of the value we cherish within the constraints of prevailing law and environment we live in. Our individual values serve important determinants of our behavior. Values serve as criteria for making decisions and determining priorities and help in explaining our justification of our own actions.

Behavioral coaching is based on the principles of behavioral science. In order to achieve genuine, lasting change in behavior, behavioral coaching capitalizes on "strategies and processes" by focusing on the behavioral components of the change program, i.e., on the behavior of the individual involved. It is important for the executive to understand initially what are their dysfunctional current behaviors and the impact of these behaviors—intended or unintended—on others and how others perceive them. Understanding these behaviors and how to change these behaviors involve exploring the dynamics of human interaction as well as understanding the personal and organizational variables.

Effective changes in behavior are significantly difficult and time consuming. It is not very uncommon to notice in organizations that the high-performing executives have one or a few areas of their behavior that hamper their career advancement or reduce their effectiveness. These could be abrasive behavior, interpersonal skills, networking, communication skills, conflict management, and lack of delegation or micro-management.

The following are some of the typical dysfunctional behaviors displayed by leaders in the organizations:

- Don't listen, interrupt others while speaking including in meeting
- Have got all answers
- "I know it all"
- Get abrasive to all including superior, colleague
- Lead, follow or get out of the way, high ego
- Procrastinate
- Poor planning, firefighting, needs follow-up
- Play favorites
- Withhold information, knowledge
- Too narrow in day-to-day working, do not predict future
- Create boundaries, functional mindsets not business mindsets
- Hesitate in discussing performance issue with subordinates
- Always under stress, get angry at workplace, poor work-life balance
- Take undue credit of subordinate work, do not project subordinates

Behavioral coaching is based on the following assumptions (Skiffington and Zeus, 2003):

1. All behaviors result in positive or negative consequences for the individual and those around him or her.
2. Behaviors that have positive consequences tend to be repeated.
3. Exploring and changing core values, motivation, beliefs and emotions can result in significant behavioral change.
4. By carefully assessing the target behaviors, learning and reinforcing new behaviors, conducting ongoing monitoring and evaluation, and maintaining behavioral change, sustained personal and organizational growth can be achieved.
5. Change involves learning and there are established laws of learning and methods whereby learning can be transferred from one situation to another.
6. Individuals are systems within systems, and each individual affects and is affected by these systems and the constant changes they are undergoing.

The ultimate goal of behavioral coaching is to effect sustainable change in an executive's behavior that improves performance. The coach helps the executive to practice new behaviors in a structured way and build up the skills gradually. Interpersonal behavior of an executive, one such example, is as crucial as performance.

Behavior Modification through Reinforcement Techniques

Behavior is the only thing any manager can deal with it. Manager can see it when it is bad, they can measure it and they can talk about it with their executives/employees. Managers can observe when it changes and can also measure it when it changes. Principles of behavior modification theory suggest that a complex pattern of behavior can be modified by first breaking it down into smaller behaviors. When the executive does goal setting, the coach encourages the executives to break the large goals into subgoals, and identify activities or actions or sub-activities to be undertaken to achieve subgoals or intermediate goals.

A reinforcer is simply any event that strengthens the behavior it follows. For example, if a child is rewarded with a candy if he doesn't disturb when his mother cooks food, then he is more likely not to disturb his mother whenever she is busy in cooking. Behaviors that are steps toward a final goal need to be reinforced and established first, with rewards given for partial accomplishment, if necessary.

Reinforcement theory is based on the basic premise that consequences influence behavior. If an executive wants to increase a behavior (say make it more frequent) the coach may provide a positive consequence (or reward) when the behavior is shown. Reinforcement could be negative also. If an executive/employee does complete the assignment within time without mistake, the supervisor may ask him not to do extra hours and can leave office early. In that case, his good behavior is negatively reinforced.

Rewards can be extrinsic (like receiving praise and encouragement from the coach or other people or receiving a gift) or intrinsic (like experiencing a feeling of accomplishment or gratification from attaining a personal milestone). If the coach is helping his executive in decreasing a particular behavior (make it less frequent), the coach may provide a negative consequence or punishment, when the behavior is shown. A behavioral coach may facilitate the executive to extinguish a behavior by providing no consequence (ignoring the behavior) when it is shown.

Behavior modification concept tells that "behavior that is followed by a positive consequence will tend to repeat itself." It suggests that people do the thing and increase the frequency of doing the same things again and again, if a positive consequence follows in each time they do that activity. However this principle only works if:

1. The consequence is to the individual.
2. The consequence is positive.
3. The consequence occurs soon after the action.

Reinforcement is an event that, when presented after a behavior, causes the behavior to increase or decrease in frequency. Anything that strengthens the behavior is reinforcer (positive or negative). Any consequence that occurs after an action and increases the frequency of that action is called a positive reinforcer. Positive reinforcement increases the likelihood of a behavior occurring again.

Behavior that is followed by a negative consequence or a painful event will decrease in frequency. Negative reinforcement refers to taking away something unpleasant. Negative consequences have two major serious side effects. When managers use negative reinforcer or create a painful event for the executive/employee to reduce a particular behavior, the executive/employee becomes apprehensive. Secondly, when executives/employees are subjected to punishment or painful events, they may decrease the frequency of behavior that is causing the painful consequence, but may also react aggressively by disruptive actions or sabotaging work. Hence it is recommended that managers should direct their attention toward increasing executive/employees' those behaviors that they want, instead of directing their energy in decreasing the executive/employees' behavior that they do not want.

Extinction means if a person is not reinforced for a behavior that was previously reinforced, he or she is less likely to act the same way when faced with a similar situation. Extinction causes a particular behavior to lessen and finally cease to occur. To strengthen new behavior, behavioral coach ensures that new behaviors are positively reinforced on an intermittent basis, rather than every time it occurs. Behavioral coaches understand the role of praise as a major source of reinforcement of the behavioral change process.

How do the coaches use reinforcement theory during the coaching process? Acknowledgment, celebration, and enthusiastic responses to the executive are some of the positive reinforcement techniques used by the coaches. On the contrary, when the executive does not keep his commitment to turn up for coaching on time, then the coach uses negative reinforcement to decrease the late-coming behavior of the executive, maybe by closing the session at the predetermined time instead of extending the coaching session. When the executive tries to go into a trap about past experiences or frequently tells unconnected stories to get undue advantage or praise from the coach, the coach uses extinction technique by ignoring the behaviors demonstrated by the executive. Normally, the situation of punishing a behavior may not arise in coaching context.

The steps listed below may be followed in using reinforcement theory into behavioral coaching scenario:

1. *Select a specific behavior to be changed:* The coach and the executive identify one specific behavior that is either to be increased or decreased or adopted. For example, an executive has a tendency to talk to his team members in meeting in a louder voice and quite fast. He would like to decrease this dysfunctional behavior.

2. *Selection of a reinforcer:* The coach and the executive choose a reinforcer that is meaningful to the executive. The selection of the reinforcer is one preferably that the executive is relatively deprived of. For example, the coach and the executive decide to start practicing to speak slowly and not to raise their voice in the coaching conversation. Whenever the executive does that the coach will praise him immediately and add a coin to the credit of his account, which entitles him for an additional session in exchange of a certain number of coins.

3. *Reinforcer is contingent for the specific behavior:* Reinforcement should be given contingent to a specific behavior not combined with other behaviors. For example, an executive normally delays specific tasks assigned to him. His supervisor may tell the executive that "whenever you submit tasks before time, I will make sure that you leave office on those days on time and not detained for urgent work."

The following case study illustrates the application of reinforcement principle in a coaching situation.

Case Study

Executive M was working as Vice President (Operations) with a mid-sized company in India. During one coaching session, he mentioned that People Management is one of the areas where he would like to work on. In the subsequent session, the Fundamental Interpersonal Relations Orientation–Behavior (FIRO-B) instrument was administered and the result highlighted that he had very low interpersonal need. His inclusion score was very low, which is a typical characteristic of a "loner."

Executive M reflected on the findings and commented that he would like to change his interpersonal behavior in the workplace because he felt that his managerial effectiveness is largely dependent on his interpersonal competency for the present role. To improve this competency, a detailed action plan was drawn, mainly covering frequency of interactions with all his subordinates and peers, mode of interactions, and areas of interactions (whether job-related or related to the well-being of his subordinates).

After a week, the coach collected random feedback from his subordinates as to whether or not they noticed any change in the behavior of their boss. If yes, what was the change and what difference had it made to them. A majority of them noticed that Executive M tried to reach out to them and they felt good about it. The coach shared these data with Executive M in the next coaching session. Executive M was happy on this feedback. He also shared how he felt during these interactions and how seriously he tried to change this behavior.

Behavioral coaches understand the importance of self-concept, self-efficacy, and self-esteem of the executive. Self-esteem indicates the extent to which the executive believes themselves to be capable, significant, successful, and worthy. Hence, behavioral coaches focus on executives' competencies, their strengths, inner talent, and past accomplishments during the coaching journey to enhance their self-efficacy.

The motivational interviewing approach, developed by Miller and Rollnick (2002) from experiences in the treatment of problem drinker, is an important approach in behavioral change process. Motivational interviewing approach focuses on identifying, exploring, and resolving ambivalence about changing behavior. It attempts to seek and to create awareness in the executive of the potential problems of their behavior and to consider what might be gained through the change. It also helps the executive examine the behavior that is not consistent with their personal values or goals. The motivational interviewing approach suggests that the ambivalence about decisions is resolved by conscious or unconscious weighing of pros and cons of changing or not changing a particular behavior. When behavioral coach uses the motivational interviewing concepts in coaching, the following four general principles are followed:

- *Express empathy:* Empathy involves seeing the world through the executive's eye, thinking about things as the executive thinks about them and feeling things as the executive feels them. Through empathic listening the coach creates an environment where the executives are more likely to share their experience honestly in an open and candid manner.

- *Develop discrepancy:* The coach develops situations in which the executive examines the discrepancies between their current behavior and future goals. When the executives realize that their current behaviors are not leading to achieving their goals, they become motivated to take up the change journey.

- *Roll with resistance:* The coach does not discuss in depth on the executive resistance but rolls with it. The coach encourages the executive to define the problem, examine the various solutions to the problem, examine different perspectives of the problems and finally develop their own solutions. In this process, the executive experiences his freedom to choose actions.

- *Support self-efficacy:* As discussed earlier, the coach keeps the executive motivated by supporting the executive's self-efficacy.

Cognitive Dissonance and Behavior Change

Cognitive dissonance refers to the state of tension that exists when a person holds inconsistent beliefs or attitudes and is motivated to reduce the dissonance. Based on the understanding of the executive's self-concept, behavioral coach would develop strategies to provide feedback to the executive and insists the executive to get feedback from others so that the executive is able to reduce inconsistency. Self-efficacy indicates the belief in our capability to organize and carry out the actions necessary to manage prospective situations. Self-efficacy influences the motivation of an individual. One will work harder and more persistently at tasks the one believes he is good at it and vice versa.

In behavioral coaching, coaches often encourage the executives to explore their own assumptions, since assumptions are at the core of behaviors; changing assumptions can, therefore, open up opportunities to use behavioral change techniques to adopt more effective behaviors.

According to cognitive dissonance theory (Festinger, 1957), there is a tendency for individuals to seek consistency among their cognitions. Cognition may be thought of as "a piece of knowledge." The knowledge may be about an attitude, an emotion, a behavior, a value, and so on. Dissonance occurs most often in situations where an individual must choose between two conflicting or incompatible cognitions. The greatest dissonance is created when the two alternative cognitions are equally attractive. Whenever there is cognitive dissonance, there is an uncomfortable tension within the person, which needs to be released either by changing his behavior or by justifying his behavior by changing the conflicting cognition, or by justifying his behavior by adding new cognitions. The following are some examples of how executives respond to feedback that is inconsistent with their self-concept:

- Discredit the source of feedback and/or the way feedback was collected
- Start refuting or argue against the feedback

- Make efforts to ensure better feedback next time
- Try to justify that the feedback is irrelevant for him
- Avoid discussing on the feedback

Another form of cognitive dissonance may surface in the coaching process if there is misalignment of individual values with the goals an executive would like to achieve or when more than one contrasting but attractive or compelling perspective emerges while reframing. If the coach observes that the executive is not taking action, or has lost interest in the goal they had chosen, it is important to explore whether or not this is due to any cognitive dissonance and, if so, how the dissonance can be reduced or removed. Executives then may either re-evaluate their personal goals in the light of the new information or perspectives, or still decide to continue to achieve their earlier set goals with more clarity even if there is a misalignment with their own values.

The following case gives an example of value incongruence.

Executive T came for coaching to get help in taking decision regarding his career transition. He was a middle-level manager of a large corporation, a talented individual, had reasonable good track record in professional work and a strong self-belief on "Karma."

He was not sure what should be his next career move. At that time, he had been working with his present employer for more than a decade and he was not very satisfied about the nature of his job. He asked his coach to facilitate him in choosing the right career. The coach elicited values of the executive through value clarification exercise. The coach assisted the executive to identify different career choices based on his background and opportunities available in the job market. After identifying the four attractive career options by the executive, the coach asked the executive to check alignment of his values with the four career options. Based on his values, the best career choice for him was to work with an NGO. The executive told his coach that he had been working for several years for under-privileged and made investment in terms of personal time and money. There was least alignment of his values with corporate career. However, the executive decided to continue with his career with corporate world, since he was in need of money to fulfill his family obligations.

Force-field analysis (Lewin, 1951) is helpful while determining if there is any discrepancy between what is actually happening and what the executive would want to happen in a given situation. In other words, which factors are assisting in the change effort (driving force) and which factors are blocking this effort (restraining force). If the driving forces far outweigh the restraining forces, the change efforts can often overpower the restraining forces. If the reverse is true, there could be different choices. If the executive realizes that it is too difficult to change, the change efforts may be given up. The change efforts may instead be continued by changing each restraining force into driving force or somehow immobilizing each of the restraining forces or focusing on driving forces and simultaneously reducing or immobilizing restraining forces. Motivation for change occurs when people perceive a discrepancy between where they are and where they want to be (Miller et al., 1992). Coaches may like to develop situations wherein the executive examines the discrepancy between their current behavior and future goals. When the executives perceive that their current behavior is not leading toward some important goals in life, they become more motivated to make important life changes.

The coach brainstorms with the executive on the payoff or advantages or disadvantages of how these new behaviors will be perceived and experienced by others with whom he works and what could be the outcomes. That is, what is driving the executive to change and what are the drivers not to change. Once these two drivers are identified, the coach helps the executive to reflect upon the reasons for change and the reasons for not to change, so that the executive ultimately feels the "pull to change."

Similarly during the goal-setting process, the coach encourages the executive to identify what strengths or favorable factors the executives possess to achieve their goals as well as the factors that may hinder executives from achieving their goals. One of the most important aspects of any coaching process is to help the executive move forward. The coach facilitates the executives in overcoming restraining forces in the journey of achieving their goals using the force-field analysis techniques.

Stages of Behavioral Change

Whitworth et al. (1998) quote, "people come to coaching because they want things to be different. They are looking for change." Whether it is executive coaching, life coaching, or any other niche areas of coaching, the bottom line is change. Hence, it is imperative to understand the behavioral change process in coaching process so that the coaches can navigate the executives effectively in the change journey. Kristine Vickers, a clinical psychologist at the Mayo Clinic in Rochester, New York, mentioned during an interview with The Wellness Councils of America, "that behavior change is more complex than just telling someone to behave differently or handing them a pamphlet. And that is why I think coaching is going to be a very important part of bringing about lifestyle change." Perry Skiffington of the Graduate School of Master Coaches (Skiffington, 2005) believes that for leaders to become or remain successful, it is required that they are able to self-manage and change their behavior at one or more of the following three levels:

1. Intrapersonal level
2. Interpersonal level
3. Organizational level

Conceptual models of change, based on over 20 years of research, suggest that behavioral change does not happen in one single step. Rather, people tend to progress through different stages on their way to successful and sustainable change. The "Transtheoretical" or famous six "stages of change" model, as proposed by Prochaska et al. (1992), was initially used in health sectors for smokers.

Prochaska et al. (1992) offer a useful change model for behavioral coaches who assist their executives to undergo behavioral change process. According to them, individuals experiencing health problems can be categorized into discrete categories (stages) on the basis of their current and past efforts to change their behavior and their intentions to change in the future. The "stages of change" model includes:

1. *Pre-contemplation:* In this stage, people are not thinking seriously about a change and are not interested in any kind of change of their behavior in the near future. On the surface, it may look that they are resisting change, but there could be several reasons for why they may be reluctant for change. They may be uninformed about the consequences of their behavior, lack confidence in their ability to change their behavior, and be defensive about others wanting them to change. It may be that people do not see themselves as having a problem. They may have tried to change on previous occasions, but were unsuccessful.

2. *Contemplation:* People in this stage acknowledge that there is a problem or an issue exists, but not yet ready or sure about making a change or make commitment to move ahead and change. They are aware of the benefits of change and also aware about the negative consequences of not changing their behavior, but procrastinate about making any move.

3. *Preparation:* People in this stage have committed to make a change and start gathering information on what resources are needed, what strategies to work on, etc. They are ready with a structured plan of action.

4. *Action:* People believe that they have the ability to change their behavior and get actively involved in taking steps to change their behavior. They have goals and action plans and have learned, practiced, and rehearsed skills and strategies to put this in place. In this stage, change of behavior is measured and evaluated.

5. *Maintenance:* The maintenance stage of change is most difficult, since many behavioral changes are not sustained over a period of time, if no process is put into place to ensure the maintenance of new behavior. To maintain the new behavior by avoiding temptation to go back to old behavior, it is important that the executive is encouraged by the coach to practice the new behavior until the new behavior becomes the second nature.

6. *Relapse:* It refers to returning to an old behavior and abandoning the changed behavior. Slipping back into an old behavior is very common, when there is a long history. Lapses and slips are part of the inevitable journey of behavioral change process. Understanding what leads to lapses and how to effectively cope with minor setbacks so that the executive does not get discouraged or disillusioned are the important issues to be handled by the coach with the executive in this stage. Each such incident is not to be considered as failure but a learning opportunity to take actions to avoid future relapse. Relapse prevention training is arranged to provide the executive to prepare for and deal with minor setbacks.

When any executive enters into a coaching relationship with a coach, the coach assesses at what stage the executive is and initiates the coaching intervention on the basis of the executive's readiness and motivation to change. Let us take a simple example of coaching intervention. When an executive is inducted into coaching by the organization, the executive is at the pre-contemplation stage, since he is not aware of any problem or that there is a need for change. When the coach or the organization conducts 360-degree feedback survey and the executive gets the survey feedback, the executive moves to the contemplation stage, wherein the executive starts thinking whether he needs to change or not, based on the feedback survey. If the executive decides that he needs to change, he is at the preparation stage. The executive then starts discussing with his coach what are the areas he needs to focus on, to improve his effectiveness, what are the options available to him and how he is going to undertake the change journey. When the executive starts taking action, he moves into action stage. After achieving success, he plans actions so that the gains achieved are not slipped back, i.e., the maintenance stage.

Table 3.1 summarizes all the concepts mentioned above within the coaching context for taking a holistic view of coaching. The

Table 3.1 Stages of Change in Coaching

Stage of Change	Coaching Context
Pre-contemplation	This is the discovery stage for the executive and focuses on the exploration of the executive's life purpose, values, and principles, where he is today, the overall satisfaction level of the executive at different aspects of life, etc. Some of the tools used by the coach here are Value Clarification, Wheel of Life, 360-degree feedback, and Questioning.
Contemplation	This is the awareness-building stage. The coaching focuses on what the executives would like to be different about their life, the choices they have, what changes they are looking for, where they are stuck, etc. Tools used by the coaches are Force-field analysis, Brainstorming, Visioning, Visualization, Gap analysis, Reframing, and Listening.
Preparation	In this stage, the executive collects information on what will be the benefits of changes, their own level of preparedness, the strengths of their desire to change, clarifying the outcomes or the goals to achieve, what strategies to be deployed, what resources are needed, what are the obstacles, and so on. The coaching tools useful in this stage are Goal setting, Brainstorming, Visualization, Gap analysis, Strength Inventory Assessment, Reframing, among others.
Action	In this stage, the executive takes action toward achieving goals. The coach assists the executive in building a system to monitor progress and take corrective actions. The tools used are Reinforcement techniques, Reviewing, Celebration, Enthusing, among others.
Maintenance	In this stage, the executive faces the challenge how to sustain the achievements or consolidate the gain or retain new behaviors. The coach assists the executive by creating structure and providing support in practicing new behavior to make it long lasting.
Relapse	This stage focuses on identification of strategy to minimize lapses to old state, to avoid taking step backward, to build self-management system and to sustain the gain without the support of the coach. The coach ends the coaching relationship here.

following two case studies briefly illustrate the different stages of the change process.

Case Example 1

Executive V was the Vice President of service function of a large dealer of construction vehicle manufacturer of India. He was managing this job for the last two years. However, he did not have any formal education in automobile engineering. During the initial exploratory phase, it emerged that he had a very high stress level, his work-life balance was exceptionally poor and he was highly concerned about his job security. His family members were insisting that he quit the job. He was virtually working 12 hours a day, seven days a week.

During the coaching sessions, each issue was analyzed, different perspectives were examined, and small steps were identified by Executive V. The progress was reasonably good, the stress level was reducing, and the executive was positive about the benefits of coaching. He was in the pre-contemplation stage of change. During subsequent sessions, it was decided that he would collect feedback from his key subordinates on two simple topics: "what he should stop doing" and "what he should continue doing."

V discussed the feedback he had received during the next coaching session. He focused on feedback regarding "delegation." While discussing the message he was getting from this feedback and how he felt about it, V concluded that he was not sure how much delegation was required from his end. Though discussion was focused on the impact of low delegation on his overall effectiveness and his role of developing subordinates, V was not sure of why, whom and how much he should delegate. This was the contemplation stage.

At that point, it was suggested by the coach whether he would like to have assessment of his managerial style. He was open to this suggestion. The Managerial Transactional Style Inventory was administered. The results from this assessment highlighted the Regulating Parent Ego state (i.e., prescriptive style) is the dominant style and non-ok style score was much higher than the ok-style score. After this intervention, followed by further enquiry and discovery, V was convinced that he was continuously trying to be at the command of his function, trying to do many things himself. He was not to able to focus on key issues due to the time constraint.

The coach explored with the executive on what he could do to reduce this dysfunctional behavior and strategies were developed. This is the preparation stage. He agreed to take action by not to be prescriptive to his subordinates about what to do in every situation but encourage them to find solutions by themselves. Even if they approach him for solutions, he would try to resist giving solution at the first instance. This was the action phase.

Contd.

Contd.

Case Example 2

Executive T was a middle-level HR executive with a large corporation in India, having 18 years of professional experience. His professional growth was limited, and he came to coaching to get assistance in making decisions regarding his career issues. During the discovery phase, value clarification, wheel of life, and inquiry/questioning tools were used to clarify the issues on which the executive would like to focus during the next four to six months at coaching sessions (this was the pre-contemplation phase of change).

During the awareness phase, the coaching process was focused on visioning, gap analysis, and reframing of perspectives, in which he was deeply engaged. Using force-field analysis techniques, the executive was encouraged to reflect on his existing behaviors and its consequence against the future vision he was formulating. The executive became aware that his existing way of life would not be enough to reach anywhere near his vision. It also emerged during this process that he was lacking in self-belief, had a fear of failure, and held a sense of complacency. He also acknowledged that procrastination was another dysfunction behavior he could not eliminate, which resulted in general laziness in all of his activities. There was visible commitment demonstrated by him to change the behavior of procrastination (he was in the contemplation phase of the change process).

During the preparation process of change, the strength inventory assessment was deployed to create a sense of self-efficacy. Value-based goals were formulated. A detailed action plan was drawn, which included milestones as well as identification of resources that were needed. The goal-setting exercise was more focused on specific actions up to the last details. One important action point was to have weekly and daily "to do" lists.

During the action phase, T took the steps that were decided in each session and shared the actions he could take and could not take, as planned. In general, the performance level was around 60 percent. But, the main focus on subsequent coaching discussion remained focused on "to do" lists, specially how to improve on performance level as well as to explore whether there was a lack of planning or the action plan was too stretched. Throughout the remaining period of coaching, planning and actions taken were the focus of conversation – to ensure that this became part of his life. The executive commented at the end of the coaching journey: "At another level, structured approach to coaching with emphasis on actions enabled me to be more action oriented. I can see the visible gains as a result of this."

Behavior Coaching Process

Observing behavior is a core component of the behavioral coaching intervention. One of the principles of behavioral coaching is to identify which specific behavior is to be changed, either to be increased or decreased or eliminated. Marshall Goldsmith (2005) states,

All of the behavioral executives that I work with use the same general approach. We first get an agreement with our coaching executives and their managers on two variables: (1) what are the key behaviors that will make the biggest positive change in increased leadership effectiveness and (2) who are the key stakeholders that should determine (one year later) if this change occurred.

The following broad process is followed by behavioral coaching intervention:

1. The coach conducts behavioral assessment using psychometric tools and/or 360-degree assessment either through survey or one-to-one interview, as discussed in the executive coaching chapter. However, the most important ingredient in the assessment tools is that the report should reflect the feedback by the raters in behavioral form, by giving ample examples of actual behavior observed or not observed. Normally, besides assessment of behavioral competencies by raters, three specific questions, "Which behavior he should continue," "Which behavior he should stop," and "Which behavior he should reduce" are asked in 360-degree assessment. Without any specific behavioral feedback, the executive will not understand which behavioral competencies he needs to change.

2. The coach presents the feedback of assessment to executives in a constructive and as a matter of facts basis, not interpreting the results of the assessment for the executive. The coach encourages the executive to reflect the feedback and assessment reports, so that he is able to identify which feedback matches with his own self-concept or self-insights of his

strengths and areas for developments and also there is gap between the feedback and the executive's own assessment.

3. The executive then identifies which behaviors he would like to work on based on the reflections he had and define clearly what he needs to change and by when. While identifying the behaviors to change, the coach encourages the executive to identify at least one functional behavior of the executive which the executive can leverage his strength while working on one or two dysfunctional behaviors. The coach may use the behavioral force-field analysis for identification of behaviors to change.

4. After identifying the behaviors to change, the coach assists the executive to develop SMART goals as well as detailed manageable multiple action steps, so that the executive is able to have quick wins in taking baby steps during the initial phase of the journey.

5. The coach assesses the readiness of the executive in the change journey and develops appropriate coaching strategies depending on whether the executive is at contemplation or preparation or action stage of the change process. As discussed earlier, the coach uses different coaching tools and skills based on the readiness of the executive.

6. The coach facilitates the behavioral change journey of the executive by providing emotional supports through enhancing their self-esteem, strengthening their self-efficacy, acknowledging their accomplishments, overcoming the barriers, monitoring the progress in the change progress, providing reinforcers as and when required, and ensuring the commitment level of the executive on the change journey.

7. When the executive is able to change his behaviors, the coach helps the executive ensure that the changes are sustained over a period of time. Assessment of change of behavior as viewed by supervisors, peers, and subordinates at workplace is conducted to compare the result of pre-coaching and post-coaching feedback.

In summary, behavioral coaching is based on the theory and practices of behavioral science. Self-efficacy, self-esteem, and self-image of the executive are explored in behavioral coaching framework. The behavioral coaching interventions involve a process of behavioral assessment of the executive, targeting behaviors for change and measurement of behavior changes. The behavioral change process is driven through various tools and techniques for behavioral modification theories.

Chapter Summary

Lasting and effective changes in behavior are difficult to achieve and time consuming. At the same time, such changes in behavior are important and necessary also. It is a common knowledge that high-performing executives have achieved success because of their strengths, in spite of having certain behavioral flaws. These limiting behaviors if taken care, the executives can significantly enhance their effectiveness.

This chapter highlights the importance of behavioral coaching intervention and the techniques involved in carrying out behavioral changes to enhance executive effectiveness. Behavioral Coaching follows certain principles, processes, and strategies to enable the executive to achieve pre-determined behavioral changes. It is important to understand the behavioral change process in the coaching process so that the coach can influence the executive effectively in the change journey.

In a joint exercise, the coach and the executive with the feedback from other stakeholders, decide which areas to focus on to improve effectiveness, what are the options available to him, and how he is going to undertake the change journey. The coach assesses at what stage of change the executive is and initiates the coaching intervention on the basis of the executive's readiness and motivation to change. He applies reinforcement techniques for the executive's behavior modification. The coach understands various

reinforcement techniques and makes use of them to impact behavioral changes. Acknowledgments, celebrations, enthuse, appreciations, etc., are some of the positive reinforcement techniques used
by the coaches. Similarly, coaches may use negative reinforcement
techniques such as extinction technique by ignoring the behavior
demonstrated by the executive. Based on the understanding of the
executive's self-concept, the behavioral coach would develop strategies to provide feedback to the executive and insist the executive
to get feedback from others so that the executive is able to reduce
inconsistency or cognitive dissonance.

In behavioral coaching, coaches encourage the executive to
explore his own assumptions, since assumptions are the core of
behaviors, changing assumptions can therefore open up opportunities to adopt more effective behaviors. Applying force-field analysis,
the coach encourages the executive to identify what strengths or
favorable factors the executive possesses to achieve the goal as well
as the factors that may hinder the executive from achieving the goal.
One of the most important aspects of any coaching process is to
help the executive to move forward. Coach facilitates the executive in overcoming restraining forces in the change journey. The
coach facilitates the behavioral change journey of the executive
by providing emotional support through enhancing self-esteem,
strengthening self-efficacy, acknowledging the accomplishments,
providing reinforcements as and when required, and ensuring the
commitment level of the executive on the change journey.

References

Festinger, L. (1957). *A theory of cognitive dissonance*. Palo Alto, California: Stanford University Press.

Goldsmith, M. (2005). Changing leadership behavior. In H. Morgen, P. Harkins, & M. Goldsmith (eds), *The art and practice of leadership coaching*, pp. 56–60. Hoboken, New Jersey: John Wiley & Sons, Inc.

Lewin, K. (1951). *Field theory in social sciences*. New York: Harper & Brothers.

Miller, R., Zweben, A., Diclemente, C.C., & Rychtarik, R.G. (1992). *Motivational enhancement therapy manual: A clinical research guide for therapist treating individual with alcohol abuse and dependence*. Rockville, Maryland: Department of Health and Health Services.

Miller, W.R. & Rollnick, S. (2002). *Motivational interviewing: Preparing people for change*, 2nd ed. New York: Guilford Press.

Prochaska, J.O., Diclemente, C.C., & Norcross, J.C. (1992). In search of how people change: Applications to addictive behavior. *American Psychologist*, 47, pp. 1102–1114.

Skiffington, P.Z. (2005). www.coachinglogic.com/Executive_life_Business_Coaching_kits.htm, accessed in December 2005.

Skiffington, S. & Zeus, P. (2003). *Behavioral coaching: How to build sustainable personal and organizational strength*. New Delhi: Tata McGraw-Hill.

Whitworth, L., Kimsey-House, H., & Sandahl, P. (1998). *Co-active Coaching: New skills for coaching people towards success in work and life*. Palo Alto, CA: Davis-Black Publishing.

CHAPTER 4

Performance Coaching
A Performance Enhancement Tool

Performance, in simple word, means getting the job done. Performance is what an executive/employee does and does not do. Organizations exist and grow, when its employees perform. If employees in an organization do not perform at the desired level, the organization does not survive. If employees perform at their peak level, the organization thrives. The performance of employees depends on various factors. However, we may broadly define performance as follows:

Employee performance = function (knowledge, skills, and abilities) × motivation × resources

Every organization would like to be and remain as a performance-driven organization. The role of managers in the corporation is not only putting right people into the right job to exploit the potential of individual executive/employee and provide necessary resources but also to create motivating environment for the executives/employees, so that the executives/employees put their best efforts to meet the expectation of the organization with respect to organization performance. Organizations invest a lot of resources, energy, and efforts in developing and implementing an effective performance management system, so that the business objectives and goals are achieved through the contributions of all executives/employees.

Effective performance management system in organizations encompasses the following key processes:

1. Performance planning or target setting
2. Performance evaluation, i.e., evaluating executive/employee performance against set standards or periodic performance review
3. Performance feedback, wherein information is exchanged between executive/employee and manager concerning the performance expected and the performance delivered
4. Performance counseling, if the performance is below the expectations

Figure 4.1 explains the performance cycle of a performance management system of an organization.

Let us discuss briefly each activity one by one. Normal practice in an organization in the performance planning phase is manager sets the targets of executives/employees based on departmental goals and objectives. It is expected that if all executives/employees work toward achieving the departmental objectives, this in turn helps the organization achieve its strategic objectives and business goals. Balanced Score Card, Key Performance Indicators, Management by Objectives, Policy Deployment, etc., are some of the tools used in

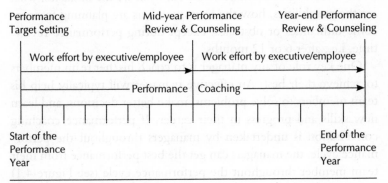

Figure 4.1 Performance Management Cycle

target setting process. If we closely look at what actually happens in any organization during performance planning phase, managers spent almost 95 percent of their time in deciding what targets to be fixed and in convincing their executives/employees on achieving these targets. In fact, negligible time is spent in discussing with executives/employees how these targets will be achieved as well as in getting the commitments from the executives/employees on the performance targets.

During performance evaluation or review phase, whether mid-term or end of the performance year, the manager reviews and evaluates the executive/employee performance against the performance plan. Hence, it is an analysis of past events after 6 or 12 months and a judgment is made about executive/employee performance based on the available performance data. Based on the evaluation of performance of employee, the manager provides performance feedback to his/her employees, so that the employees are able to know whether they are on track or not. Again, the performance feedback is based on the evaluation of achievement of performance targets against performance plan, not much on how to improve or enhance performance. If any employee meets his/her targets, he/she is acknowledged, else performance counseling is done if the performance is below the expectation.

Generally, no significant conversation is undertaken by the manager with their team members during the whole performance period on how the targets are to be achieved, what are the obstacles, what are the possibilities, how the team members are planning to overcome difficulties or obstacles, except during performance review time, i.e., after 6 or 12 months.

One key role of any manager is to coach his/her team members to achieve their best. An effective manager will typically help his team members to solve problems, make better decisions, and learn new skills and progress in their career. If performance coaching conversation is undertaken by managers throughout the performance cycle, the managers can get the best performance from their team member throughout the performance cycle (see Figure 4.1) by engaging with the team in every step of performance.

Awareness and responsibility are the key principles of coaching. Whitmore defined awareness as "knowing what is happening around you" while self-awareness is "knowing what you are experiencing." Responsibility is concerned with personal choice and control. Choice implies freedom. If managers give responsibility to their executives/employees, the executives/employees, in turn, will try to put their best efforts. The goal of performance coaching is to transform the business by transforming the person. The performance coach (manager) supports their executives to attain a set of stretched goals. The emphasis of performance coaching process is on creating a personalized plan of the executive by helping the executive finds answers to the existing challenges, obstacles, and dilemmas.

Let us look into another aspect of performance of employees. Every organization conducts monthly performance review meetings, at business level, functional levels, departmental levels, or team levels. These meetings are either conducted for a whole day or for two to three hours in every month. If you are one of the members of such meetings, you will agree with me that around 90 percent of time is normally spent on reviewing what are not achieved and why not achieved, which is just post-mortem. I am not, by any means, saying it is not important. It is also important to estimate how much time we, the managers, are spending on planning for the next month's performance and discussing how the targets will be achieved as compared to analyzing and reviewing last month's performance during these review meetings.

Whether you are sales manager or production manager, managing a team, one proven performance coaching tool that can help you deal with performance issue of your team member is the GROW model. GROW is an acronym standing for **G**oal—**C**urrent **R**eality—**O**ptions—**W**ill. The GROW model is a simple yet powerful framework for structuring a performance coaching session. The GROW model was originally developed by Graham Alexander in 1984 and popularized by John Whitmore. The early practitioner of coaching used a similar process of GROW more or less intuitively. The GROW model gives a certain sequence of questioning at key stages of coaching conversation. The originators saw that, just as in sport, many individuals were struggling to achieve their goals because they were not learning from their own experiences and were not aware of the knowledge they have within themselves that would help them.

The GROW model enables the manager to break down a major performance issue into several sub-issues, which are easy to address in developing solutions. The GROW model not only helps individual to take action but also shows how to take action in the most effective way. The basic framework of the GROW model is as follows:

- **G—G**oals   >   What do you **want**?
- **R—R**eality   >   What is **happening** now?
- **O—O**ptions   >   What **could** you do?
- **W—W**ill   >   What **will** you do?

The principle behind the GROW process is rooted in the Inner Game theory developed by Timothy Gallwey, a tennis coach who was frustrated by the limitations of the conventional sports coaching methods. He noticed that he could often see the faults in a player's game, but that simply telling him what to do to improve did not bring about lasting change.

For instance, if a player was not keeping his eye on the ball, most coaches would give advice such as: "Keep your eye on the ball." When a player received this sort of instruction he would try to do what the coach was asking him and watch the ball more closely. Unfortunately, no one can keep instructions in the front of their minds for long. So the player usually slips back into his old habits and both the coach and the player grow increasingly frustrated.

So one day, instead of giving an instruction, Gallwey asked: "Can you say 'bounce' out loud when the ball bounces and 'hit' out loud when you hit the ball?"

In order to do this, the players had to keep their eyes on the ball but no longer had a voice in their heads repeating the words "I must keep my eye on the ball." At this, their play started to improve markedly and the Inner Game method of coaching was born. From then on, whenever Gallwey wanted a player to change, he no longer gave instructions but would, instead, ask questions that would help the player discover for himself what worked and what needed to change.

A number of principles have been developed out of Gallwey's experience with tennis players. While the Inner Game theory originated from sport, the same principles are applied to business situations. The best learning happens when we are focusing on the present and make discoveries as we go along. While the Inner Game was developed in sport, the coaches using it realized that it could also be applied in other learning situations.

Sir John Whitmore, bestselling author of the book *Coaching for performance* was born in the UK in 1937, underwent his education in Military College and Agricultural College. His initial passion was in motor sports, and he won the European Car Championship. He left motor racing shortly after that, and started running a large agribusiness, a product design business, and a Ford dealership. Though he had material success both from racing and from business, he was not satisfied. Sir John Whitmore was also deeply influenced by the Gallwey approach and got himself trained by Gallwey in Inner Game and returned to the UK to represent Inner Game in Europe.

Whitmore and a group of British coaches including Graham Alexander and Caroline Harris set up The Inner Game Limited and ran courses in late 1979 and early 1980 for tennis and skiing. However, enquiries from business world started coming to Whitmore and his colleagues on the potential application of inner game concept in the work environment. Since Whitmore viewed The Inner Game as the purest basis of workplace coaching, he trained business executives on Gallwey principles of coaching. As the concept of coaching was becoming popular in the UK, Whitmore dropped the Inner Game name and started calling coaching. He wrote a book on "Coaching for Performance," which became bestseller in the field. Whitmore believes that it is important to recognize and eliminate our internal obstacles and fear is the greatest of those obstacles.

The word "Inner" was used by Timothy Gallwey as "the opponent within one's own head is more formidable than the one the other side of the net." As per the Inner Game theory, a person has two selves, Self One and Self Two.

Self One, "the conscious teller," is the internalized voice of our parents, teachers, and those in authority. Self Two, "the unconscious doer," is the whole human being with all its potential and capacities including the "hard-wired" capacity to learn. It is characterized by relaxed concentration, enjoyment, and trust. Self One seeks to control Self Two and does not trust it. Self One is characterized by tension, fear, doubts, and trying too hard.

The key to better anything, whether tennis or any other sport or performance at workplace, lies in improving the relationship between Self One and Self Two. Thinking activity of Self One creates interferences with the natural doing processes of Self Two. One's peak performance is achieved when the mind is quiet and there is harmony between the two selves. Myles Downey, one of the disciples of Timothy Gallwey, hence quoted, "Potential minus interference is equal to performance."

Gallwey claimed that if a coach can help a player remove or reduce the internal obstacles to their performance, an unexpected natural ability will flow without the need for input from the coach. Whitmore defined coaching based on the essence of Gallwey as, "Coaching is unlocking a person's potential to maximize their own performance. It is helping them to learn rather than teaching them."

Let us now explore how the GROW model can help managers deal with performance issues at the workplace.

G is for Goal.

What does the executive really want?

In any coaching conversation, the performance coach (or manager) generally starts the coaching session by asking the executive what he would like to focus on during the coaching session. It is important for the coach to get clarity on what the executive really wants. Normally, the executive may not be very clear at the beginning what actually they want or what they would like to focus on in the coaching session.

After getting clarity on the issues the executive would like to discuss with the coach, the next important step for the coach is to find out from the executive the outcomes or goals they want to achieve. If there is no clarity on the goals or outcomes the executive wants to achieve, then the coaching conversation becomes directionless. The goals are where the coaching actually begins. It is possible that the executive may not be very clear of the goals or have difficulty in articulating the goals they want to achieve. The coach assists the executive to decide what they really want to achieve at their workplace or what is important for their success and happiness in their life. It is important in life to know "where is the goalpost."

Sometimes, the end goal may be very big and far, but to achieve the end goal, some important milestones require to be identified during this stage. Let us take one example. One young executive of mine wanted to join the public services and wanted to be minister in the state government of India in the coming five years. One milestone identified during coaching was to be a member of legislative state assembly by the next two years. To achieve this milestone, it emerged that he should actively get involved with mainstream politics and try to get nomination from a particular party for the state legislative election. However, the legislative election was due only after three years, and he decided to keep one milestone of getting a nomination and fighting election in the next three years.

Let me take another example. One of my executives, aged around 58 years, who was working with a public sector company, came to coaching for planning post-retirement career option. One of the issues that cropped up during one of the coaching sessions was he was trying to reduce his weight for a long time but was not successful. Not only was this issue bothering him quite a lot recently but he also received strong medical advice to take action on this front. So, during the coaching session he decided to reduce at least 5 kg in the next six months. During further deliberation on this goal, he took target of reducing his weight by 2 kg initially by January 1 (which was two and half months from that day), the target date of achieving this milestone.

In some situations, the executives may not have full control of the result they are aiming at, but to achieve the end goal, the executive is expected to take several actions or activities. Each such activity or process will have the goals; achievement of these process goals will make the executive move forward toward the end goals. In the previous example, the executive did not have his control of winning the election but he could take action of at least getting a nomination to fight election by getting actively involved in political mainstream.

It is very common to find that most executives struggle at choosing clear, specific and achievable goals for an agreed timeframe. Whether in life, career, or workplace coaching issue, the role of the performance coach is to assist the executive to clearly and specifically identify the goals that pull them. In fact, many executives discover their goals during the coaching discussion. Performance coach helps his/her coachee define a goal that is specific, measurable, and realistic.

There is a system to create goals. To just say we want something is not enough. There is an acronym that is often used to describe powerful goals that assist the coach and the executive to evaluate whether the goals are thoroughly thought through. The goals should be S.M.A.R.T.E.R. It stands for:

Specific: Specific means the goals are concrete, detailed, focused, and well-defined. Just saying we want to reduce wastage or reduce weight is not enough. We need to be specific how much wastage percentage to be achieved or what is the weight we should achieve.

Measurable: Goals must be measurable. If the goal is not measurable, then how it will be known whether it is achieved or not achieved. Moreover, measurable goals help the executive track the progress toward the goals. Measurement could be quantitative as far as possible. We may measure the goal of wastage reduction in terms of percentage of waste generated.

Achievable: Goals should be stretchable but achievable. If the goal is too far and out of reach, then it will be difficult to keep the executive motivated and strive for it. For example, if the present wastage level, say, is 6 percent and the executive fixes the goal as 2 percent, which was never achieved at the recent past, then it is not an achievable target.

Realistic: Goals should be realistic. Setting a goal may be realistic but there may be different influencing factors for achieving the goal. For example, in the example of waste reduction, though it may look like that 2 percent waste level is achievable, there could be many influencing factors like product–mix, production plan, and demand and process parameters.

Time bound: By when the goal has to be achieved? By one month, three months, or six months? If the time horizon is too long, then the executive may lose focus. If it is too short, then it could be difficult to achieve. Realistic time frame creates the necessary urgency in the mind of the executive to take prompt actions.

Exciting: The goal must be engaging for the individual. When the executive is excited by the goal or the journey, they are more likely to engage themselves in the achievement of the activity being discussed. In organization, some managers just decide the team targets without much discussion and ask the team to work for the target. Though it is the responsibility of team manager to set team targets, the ownership of the targets only could be achieved if the team members were involved during fixing goals.

Rewarding: Executives should know what it will mean to them, why it is important for them, and what will be the results and personal benefits for them in achieving the goal.

The following useful questions are asked in setting goals:

- What is the aim of discussion?
- What do you want to achieve in the long term?
- What does success look like?

- How much personal control or influence do you have over your goal?
- What would a milestone be on the way?
- What is the short-term goal on the way?
- By when do you want to achieve it ?
- Is that possible, challenging, and attainable?
- How will you measure it?
- How will you know that you have achieved that goal?
- How will you know the problem is solved?

The following points are to be kept in mind while fixing goals:

1. The goals are to be stated in the positive, instead of the negative. Remember "The Law of Attraction."
2. Turn the goals into positive affirmations.
3. The goals need to be agreed upon and recorded. If there is no buy-in by the executives/employees or team members, then the executive/employee will not take ownership and responsibility.

R is for Reality.

If the goal is the final destination, the reality is where the executive is currently at. After defining goals, the next important phase of performance coaching is to get clarity of the current situation, i.e., taking stock of where the executive is and what he/she has. It means how far the executive is from the goals. No goals can be achieved unless the current situation is known and understood. It should also include all the resources the executive might have and they would like to use as well as what are the obstacles they may face to achieve their goals. In corporations, most of the reality questions are the facts and figures of present performance, past occurrences, actions taken, resources available, the obstacles overcome, etc. Most reality questions are asked by using "What," "How much," "When," "Where," "Who," etc.

In this stage of coaching conversation, ask your team members to describe their current reality. This is a very important step. Too often, people try to solve a problem without fully considering their starting point. Often they are missing some of the information they need to solve the problem effectively.

The other part of the reality questions covers the resources, viz., skills, equipment, money, contacts, supports, knowledge, expertise, etc., the executive might use or they have at their disposal, even if the things that do not appear to be useful at first sight. There will certainly be certain obstacles or road blocks that may prevent the executive to move from where they are now to where they want to be. It is also important to identify all the obstacles that stand in the way. The purpose of questioning is not to find solutions to overcome the obstacles but identify all possible obstacles in achieving their goals or resources the executive does have and does not have.

Useful coaching questions include:

- What is happening now?
- *(What, when, where, who, how much, how often)*
- Who is involved (directly and indirectly)?
- What resources do you have?
- What happens to the others directly involved?
- What is the effect on others?
- What have you done about this so far?
- What is missing in the situation?
- What is the affect or result of that?
- What is stopping you?
- What resources you do not have?
- What could be roadblock?
- Whom you can depend on?
- What are the challenges you could foresee?

O is for Options.

The purpose of this stage is to create a list of as many as possible alternative actions possible or available. The coach brainstorms with the executive so that the executive is able to find many options to reach the milestones and end goals. Some of the best breakthroughs will come from a totally fresh point of view. Therefore, the quantity of options is important initially than the quality of each option. Some options may be relevant to move forward, some may be to remove obstacles, and some could be for turning the obstacles into assets. The coach facilitates the process by providing a motivating environment to the executive so that the executive thinks creatively for finding various options. Sometimes, the executive may not come with new options after listing some options. It is quite natural. The executive may list options that are most obvious choices but not necessarily the best choices. Hence, the coach keeps patience during this process and allows the executive to think for more options. The coach may give some clues or asks some leading questions so that the executive may start thinking new options, which he might have not thought earlier. To create options, the coach may take each obstacle in turn and ask the executive what and how this obstacle can be overcome.

The following are some questions that can be asked to create options:

- What are the options you have?
- What else could you do?
- Anything else?
- If you have enough *Time, power, money, etc., what will you do?*
- Would you like to think another option?
- What are the benefits and cost of each?
- How will you tackle this constraint?
- What are the benefits and downsides of this option?
- What factors will you use to weigh up the options?
- If this option does not work, what will you do?

When the coach is brainstorming with the executive, the executive may exhaust ideas or not think in the most obvious direction. Sometime, the executive may ask advice from coach or point of views of the coach. The coach is generally very careful in providing their own opinion or advice. When I do performance coaching with my coachees (who are not my subordinates), I will normally resist to provide my point of view till no new idea is coming from the executive or the executive gets stuck. I will offer my idea just as my opinion which the executive may like to explore. I may start by saying like this, "… well, I may suggest couple of alternatives which you may like to explore. However, it may or may not work with you, but it worked in similar situations like this." I will keep my suggestion on the table for the executive to examine it with other alternatives and never get attached to my suggestions. I insist on my coachee that my idea is just as a lead and he needs to think more ideas for his situation.

W is for Will or Way Forward.

The last stage of GROW is identifying the Way Forward. The purpose of this stage is to narrow down the options available to the executives, evaluate each option, and then decide on the action plan to achieve the goals. By examining current reality and options available, the executive will have a reasonable idea how to move forward, as the executive selected different options that will achieve the goal. The Way Forward step should be concrete, specific, and time bound so that the executive is clear what the specific steps are to be taken to move toward their goals.

In the final step in this stage, the role of the coach is to ensure that the executive is committed to take specific actions. In doing so, the coach will help the executive strengthen their will and motivation.

The following are examples of some questions, which may be asked in this stage:

- Which option or options did you choose?
- What are you going to do?
- To what extent does this meet all your objectives?

- What obstacles you might meet along the way?
- What are your criteria and measurements for the success?
- When precisely are you going to start and finish each step?
- When are you going to take first step?
- Will this action meet your goal?
- What could hinder you in taking your first steps?
- What personal resistance do you have, if any, to taking these steps?
- What would you do to eliminate these external and internal factors?
- Who needs to know what your plans are?
- What support do you need and from whom?
- What will you do to obtain that support and when?
- What could I do to support you?
- Rate on a 1–10 scale that you are confident that you will take the agreed actions.
- What commitment on a 1–10 scale do you have to take these agreed actions?
- What prevents this from being a 10?

Sometimes, the coach needs to explore with the coachee of each option extensively before the executive is able to make their final choices of action. It is possible to revisit sometimes the goals and/or obstacles, decided at previous steps, to refine or realign the actions with the goals. It may require revising the goals and/or milestones, revisit the resources needed, or check whether all obstacles identified are relevant now.

The power of GROW model is that it is easy to understand, straightforward to apply, and has a very thorough process of enquiry. In addition, once someone has developed an understanding of how it works, it is possible to apply it to a variety of work-related performance issues, even complex multi-faceted ones, in a very effective way. It often enables individuals to make progress on issues even when they have been stuck for a long time. For most managers, GROW offers an excellent tool to engage in leadership activities in the process of achievement of departmental objectives. The following two coaching case scenarios give some idea of using the GROW model of performance coaching in the coaching conversation.

Coaching Scenario 1

Coach: What would you like to discuss today?

Executive: I would like to discuss with you my performance target for this year. Our yearly sales planning activity was just finished last week. My sales target has been doubled as compared to the last year. I am thinking about what I should do.

Coach: Well, you would like to discuss what you should do to meet the higher sales target for the year. Before going for that, let me understand whether this target is achievable.

Executive: The market opportunity is large, we are only catering a small part of it. It is possible to achieve target but quite stretched for me to just double the number in twelve months.

Coach: Well, I hear that you are quite optimistic about your new challenge. Let us discuss what are the targets you have fixed for yourself for coming four quarters.

Executive: I am thinking a lot about this. I am thinking to break the increased volume in the ratio of 20:20:30:30. for four quarters.

Coach: Any specific reasons?

Executive: I need to work for additional target quite aggressively in the first quarter. I am not confident that it will convert into sales in the first quarter, but definitely will reflect from second quarter onwards. The peak business sessions in our business are always in the last two quarters i.e., the third quarter being the festive season and the last quarter being winter time and the end of financial year of most organizations. That is why I kept higher volume targets for the last two quarters.

Coach: To achieve your increased targets, what are the resources you have and what resources you need?

Executive: We have strong database of potential customers. My management has promised me all supports including additional sanction of sales promotion expenditure in my area. I need to submit budget proposal

Contd.

for this by next week. Presently I have four members in my team who directly involved in front-end sales and two employees at the back office. I am thinking to add two more people in my team.

Coach: Do you have sanction to add two members in your team?

Executive: No.

Coach: To add two new members in your team what are the actions you need to take?

Executive: First, I need to get approval of increase of manpower from my boss, then send it to HR. If there is any internal candidate who can be transferred, then it could be done fast else it will require at least two weeks to add new member in my team.

Coach: What can be done to make it fast? As I am hearing from you, it may require four weeks at minimum.

Executive: I will send the manpower requisition by tomorrow. I will speak to my counterparts in other regions as well as Manager (HR) to find out in the meantime, if any internal candidate is possible. I know some ex-employees of this organization, who wanted to join back this organization.

Coach: Great! You now have some important and urgent tasks in your hand. Assume you have your additional resources by the next three weeks, what you are going to do different than what you normally do to achieve your target.

Executive: I am thinking about entering into two new market segments, where our presence is minimal. One is Real Estate and the other is Education. However, our present major focus on financial sector will continue. My two new resources will only focus in these two new segments.

Coach: So you are looking for new resources who have some domain knowledge and experience.

Executive: Ideally, yes.

Coach: What are the obstacles you could visualize to enter in these new segments?

Executive: Since we are not significantly present in these segments, there will be some difficulty in making entry. However, once we break the ice, I am confident that we can capture large businesses based on our credentials in other sectors.

Coach: For making entry into these segments, what are actions required from your end?

Executive: First, I will ask our back office team to list potential customers based on their size, then I will shortlist 40–50 such customers. After

Contd.

that our back office team will do further work on these customers and fix appointments for us to make visit.

Coach: How long time is required to complete these work and start meeting customers in these new segments ? Can you put a target date?

Executive: Well, I think by 20th of this month, we should open the door for at least five new customers.

Coach: What else could you do to meet the new targets?

Executive: We will try to increase the volume with our existing customers, though it is not very easy. I will explore whether we can get some turnkey jobs.

Coach: Anything else can you think you could do?

Executive: I think my cup is full now. Lot of work is to be done in the next fifteen days.

Coach: I agree. I am thinking about government sector including public sector organizations.

Executive: Well, we have not done much in this segment though the opportunities are big but we need to go through tendering process, which are generally long and tedious.

Coach: Would you like to explore this sector?

Executive: Not a bad idea.

Coach: What can be done in this segment?

Executive: I will ask my back office team to scan through the tender announcement henceforth and show me so that I can decide which tender we should participate.

Coach: Ok. Is there anything else you want to talk about now or are we finished for today?

Executive: Let me start taking actions what we discussed so far and then I will discuss further. Enough is for today's session. Thanks.

Coaching Scenario 2

Coach: What would you like to discuss today?

Executive: Well, I am reflecting on my life of wheel, I am fairly satisfied except two areas.

Coach: What are the two areas?

Executive: Fun and recreation, Money.

Coach: How can I help you?

Contd.

Contd.

Executive: I would like to discuss with you on the area of fun and recreation, which I was thinking about quite a lot for the last seven days.

Coach: Well, I appreciate your commitment. Let me understand from you why fun and recreation is so important for you now.

Executive: I want to be happy and cheerful both at my workplace and home. If I am happy and relaxed, I can spread happiness all around through actions and words at workplace.

Coach: What do you want to achieve in short term and long term?

Executive: Well, I would like to achieve at least 8 out of 10 in the level of satisfaction index by the next three months and 9 out of 10 by the next six months.

Coach: Where are you now?

Executive: I am at 6 or may be 6.5 now.

Coach: Great! Do you have any intermediate milestone?

Executive: I am thinking to keep it as 7.5.

Coach: Excellent! When do you want to achieve this milestone?

Executive: By the end of next month, i.e., the end of October, i.e., around 45 days from now.

Coach: Is it possible and attainable?

Executive: I think so, though it is difficult but I think I can achieve this.

Coach: What is happening now?

Executive: Because of paucity of time, I am not able to spend time in recreational activities, as I was to do earlier.

Coach: Anything else is happening with you now?

Executive: The work culture as well as work environment in my present place of posting are not conducive enough for me to have some free time.

Coach: So? How is it affecting you?

Executive: I am sometimes quite tense, which is affecting both of my work and personal life.

Coach: How are you going to manage your time?

Executive: I will manage time judiciously. I will try to leave my workplace everyday by 6 pm, except in cases when some senior person visit site from HO and meeting continues after 6 pm. In that situation, I will not have any control on my time.

Coach: How many times, on an average, it happens in a month?

Executive: Generally four to five times in a month.

Coach: How will you know you are managing time judiciously ?

Executive: By how many times in a week I punched out by 6.00 pm.

Coach: Nice. Do you think there is anything stops you in implementing this action?

Contd.

Contd.

Executive: Sometimes, unplanned events happen in my workplace like major breakdown or some urgent information need to be sent to HO.

Coach: How many times it happened in the last two months?

Executive: Twice.

Coach: What are others things you would like to do?

Executive: I would like to spend quality time with my family members.

Coach: What else you would like to do?

Executive: I will start appreciating even small things of others.

Coach: Like?

Executive: If my team member does good work or complete work without follow-up from me or able to complete maintenance work before the time, etc. Even it could be at home also. I normally do not appreciate my wife whatever she does.

Coach: Anything else you would like to do?

Executive: I will interact more with my relatives, friends and colleagues, whom I used to spend quite lot of time. I will keep reading more books on management and self-help. I will read the book "Secret," which I heard a lot about it.

Coach: What strengths or resources do you have?

Executive: My strong desire and support of my family.

Coach: What is the first action you are going to take?

Executive: Appreciate small things. I will start from home first.

Coach: From when?

Executive: By today.

Coach: What second action you would like to take?

Executive: Manage my time efficiently. I think if I can effectively manage my time in my office, then I will have enough personal time, so that I can pursue my hobbies, spend time with family and friend.

Coach: How much you are committed on both the actions? What could hinder you to take action?

Executive: I am quite passionate about both the actions. Distraction would not affect my resolve. I will remain focused on both the actions.

Coach: What will you do when first milestone is achieved?

Executive: I will celebrate with my wife. She is going to be accountability partner for me in this.

Coach: What are you going to tell me in our next session after 15 days?

Executive: How many times I have reached home by 6 pm and how many appreciations I have given to others.

Coach: It looks very exciting. All the best.

Chapter Summary

Every organization would like to develop performance-driven culture, wherein each employee puts his best efforts in meeting performance expectations of the organization, so that organizations strive in a competitive environment. In a traditional performance management system, the manager is expected to set the performance targets for their employees, review performance at the end of performance cycle, and provide performance feedback to the employees. In performance coaching, the manager assists their employees to decide the targets to be achieved, identify the actions to be taken to achieve the targets, identify the challenges or obstacles in the process, and how to overcome the challenges. Performance coaching technique is based on Inner Game theory, postulated by Timothy Gallwey, who claimed that if a coach can help a player remove or reduce internal obstacles (the opponent within one's own head) to their performance, an unexpected natural ability will flow within the player to achieve the performance. Sir John Whitmore believes that it is important to recognize and eliminate our internal obstacles, fear being the greatest of internal obstacles. Performance coaching emphasizes creating awareness and responsibility in the mind of the employee. GROW (Goal, Reality, Option, and Way Forward) model of performance coaching is an effective tool for managers to support their employees to attain a set of stretched goals by helping them find their own answers to the existing challenges, obstacles, or dilemmas, rather than directing, instructing, or controlling their performance.

CHAPTER 5

Developing Leadership Competencies through Leadership Coaching

What Is Leadership?

While there are many definitions of leadership in the literature, the most common theme is that the role of leader is to propel others toward the achievement of defined organizational goals. Hence, the effective leader should be able to balance concern for task with the concern for people. Leadership is an influencing process. Anytime you (leaders) are trying to influence the behavior of someone toward some goal, you are engaging in leadership (Blanchard, 2005). Leadership is also a relationship between those who aspire to lead and those who chose to follow (Kouzes, 2005). Leaders should have authenticity, i.e., displaying authentic behavior, "Walk the talk." Leaders should ask themselves—Who am I? What is really important for me and for others? In other words, what are the values, beliefs, attitude I carry to the work place. Credibility is the foundation of leadership. Behaviorally, credibility is "Do what you say you will do" (Kouzes, 2005). Some leaders are not clear of their own values—what is really important for them. They generally operate not in alignment with their personal values. Majority of leaders as they reach a higher echelon of management, there is a feeling of insecurity and loneliness as it becomes difficult for them to talk to others about their issues and concerns. Loneliness and isolation are perhaps the greatest challenges leaders face today. The greatest challenge for leaders of mid-sized firms seems to be making the transitions from a do-it-all micro-manager to a leader with productive followers. Effective leaders are always experimenting and taking risks by constantly generating small wins and learning from mistakes (Kouzes, 2005). Leaders need to be courageous to confront the dark corners where so much of their dysfunction resides, and to become someone fundamentally different in overcoming those handicaps (Siegal, 2005).

Transition from Managerial Role to Leadership Role

The major functions of leadership are strategic, looking business as a whole and having a global mindset. These functions differentiate leaders from managers who are primarily responsible for planning, organizing, and controlling of tasks. High-performing managers in many organizations made rapid progress in their early career due to their strong technical competencies or financial acumen, but hit the corporate ceiling due to the lack of right skill sets, so essential once they go up the corporate ladder. All managers eventually find that certain strengths that were extremely valuable early in their careers can become powerful liabilities with a rise in level and responsibility. At the same time, there are always one or two weaknesses that become increasingly exposed and exaggerated (Conger, 2005). The skills required at higher levels of management range from the ability to handle interpersonal relationships, the ability to manage a team, how to delegate, or manage change.

The leadership competencies they lack are:

Integrity and trust that showed up in whatever they do

Organizational agility and political savvy

Lack of passion

Inability to inspire others

Lonely at the top syndrome

Ability to think strategically and innovatively

Understanding organizational dynamics

Some of the typical functional behaviors the leader, more so for the manager, who moves to leadership role, need to be acquired/ enhanced are:

Focusing on macro-management

Visioning, looking beyond

Looking at business as a whole rather functional mindset

Exploiting best potential from their reportee

Influencing, motivating, challenging his team members

Strategic thinking, planning for future, anticipate futures

Commercial acumen, reading numbers, seeing trends

Outward looking than inward looking

Networking with significant others, market/customer focused

Challenge conventional wisdom

Walk the talk

But how do organizations develop leaders? Traditional leadership development programs have proved that the learning methods are limited, since development of leadership competency requires a much more extensive action learning environment, where the agenda is based on the issues the organizations are facing. However, acquiring or developing new competencies of employees can be quite challenging, more so at senior levels. Developing competencies in executives/employees is much more than transferring knowledge or teaching job skills to help them in performing their role effectively. It encompasses the executive/employee's ability to self-learn, create self-awareness, enhance his self-esteem and self-confidence, and motivate to grow and excel. Leadership development needs to focus on the need of the leader, so that an environment is created for a safe space for reflection and learning, at his/her own pace and style.

What Leadership Coaching Does?

Leadership coaching is one of the most effective methods to build leadership capabilities within an organization, besides helping leaders in achieving breakthrough results in a challenging environment. Leadership coaching is for highly achievement-oriented people, who are quite effective in their roles, but want to improve their leadership skills. Today, leaders are much more eager to learn new skills and competencies to face everyday challenges in an ever-changing competitive global environment. These leaders are aware of their weaker areas, but not sure of how to strengthen it. They would like to partner with leadership coach from outside the organization in order to brainstorm critical decisions, to receive feedback, and to get different perspectives with the coach.

Leadership coaching encompasses enhancing ability to develop trust, increasing accountability within the organization, developing satisfactory relationship with board, shareholders, and other stakeholders, enhancing credibility and influence as an ambassador, increasing the ability to align employees to the company's vision and mission, navigating change management projects, enhancing managerial competencies, and creating a culture of learning and development.

Leadership coaching can help anyone, either already in leadership position or in transition to leadership role, in building leadership capabilities, leveraging their strengths, and assisting them in achieving their leadership objectives. Leadership coaching is increasingly being used for individuals being groomed for promotion or for an individual promoted in a new position to develop leadership competencies to complement technical expertise, viz., developing competencies on communicating strategic vision, strategic planning, culture change, ambassadorship, leading executive teams, overcoming isolation, and interpersonal skills.

Leadership coach helps the leaders to understand themselves more fully so that they can draw on their strengths and use them more effectively and improve their identified development needs. In the present time, senior managers in global organizations are expected to provide leadership in increasingly diverse and dynamic environments, since they face more demands to create, implement, and manage changes effectively in a much shorter time span than it was just one decade earlier. Leaders now are not continuously searching for innovative ways to change, grow, and improve.

High-performing organizations undertake leadership coaching intervention to develop leadership pipelines within the organization. The key questions these organizations are constantly asking themselves are:

1. Do our current and high-potential leaders currently possess the core leadership skills and competencies required to fulfill our organizational strategic objectives?
2. How do we grow and strengthen the leadership pipeline within the leadership framework in the organization?
3. To what extent our organization is committed to creating a culture that will grow and sustain the required leadership competencies?

Leadership coaching focuses on both the transformational and transactional challenges of the leader. Coaching leaders for transformational change involve changing the very way they think, improving their ability to deal with ambiguity, and enhancing their creativity. This increases the individual's capacity to step back and reflect on assumptions about such things as organizational culture, core values, organizational objectives, and vision that were previously taken for granted. The transactional challenges are in achieving the strategic objectives and business goals in a highly unpredictable competitive market scenario by the leaders.

Leadership coaching, therefore, addresses issues related to enhancement of leadership competencies, styles, and behaviors as well as improving business results in alignment with the strategic objectives of the organization. Hence, the leadership coaching process is quite distinct from executive and performance coaching processes discussed earlier in this book. The reasons being that leadership coaching is deployed for a very few numbers of managers, who are already high achievers in their functional domain and reached a significant higher echelon of management hierarchy.

Leadership Coaching Process

- *Preparatory phase:* When an organization initiates leadership coaching intervention for their key executives, the organization takes utmost care in selecting the right leadership coach for their executives and ensures that the coach understands the expectations of the organization in the coaching process, the context of the working of the executive, and there is proper chemistry between the executive and the coach.

- *Assessment:* Traditional 360-degree assessment (generally 360-degree interview), shadow coaching, competency assessment centre data, performance data, growth trajectories of the leader in the organization, and executive/employee engagement index of the leader are some of the sources of data for the leadership coach to understand where the leader is now. In general, leadership coaches focus mostly on transformational issues of the leaders, since these leaders are generally successful in their role and known as achievers in their functional domain. Hence, the leadership coaching focuses on development of leadership competencies, which encompass their leadership styles and behavior. Leadership coach uses various psychometric tools and inventories, viz., MBTI, VIA Inventory of Strengths, LEAD, LSI, Value Clarification exercise, 360-degree assessment, EQ-i inventory, Hogen Personality Inventory, etc., in the diagnostics process. During the initial phase of assessment, the coach works with the executive to do the following:

- *Create a leadership map:* It is a process of developing a full picture of a person's authentic leadership. In this stage, the executives get deeper insight into their leadership journey to date by crystallizing personal and professional defining moments to understand their greatest strengths, their leadership potential and aspirations, and the path they need to take to get there. An engaging discussion between the coach and the executive helps the coach understand the evolution of the executive as a leader, what they want to be, the goals they aspire to achieve, and the strengths they have to leverage to get there. While doing so, the coach helps the executive to define their purpose, vision, values, strengths, and goals.

- *Value clarification:* In a coaching scenario, the value clarification process entails a type of Socratic dialogue in which a person is urged to reflect on his life experiences and to clarify his own values. The following steps are recommended in conducting the value clarification exercise with the executive (Mukherjee, 2011):

Step 1: First the coach has to decide the appropriate time in the coaching journey to take up this exercise. If the coach introduces this exercise in the initial stage of coaching relationship, the executive may not be ready for this exercise. It is also possible that the coach might not have developed the desired trust level with the executive and/or the coach may not have adequate opportunity to know the executive with respect to where the executive is at present, what are his challenges, his beliefs and assumptions, his life journey as well as his past experiences. Proper rapport with the executive is a prerequisite for an effective and meaningful value clarification exercise. It is therefore advisable that the coach may take the value clarification exercise when the coach has sufficient understanding about the executive's situation, sometime at the middle of the coaching journey, say after six to eight coaching sessions.

Step 2: The next important step for the coach is to check whether the executive is ready for clarifying his values by gauging the interest level of the executive before starting the exercise. Some executives just do the exercise as the coach has asked them to do, whereas others take this exercise very seriously and do a lot of reflection before coming out with their list of values. Their energy, their voice, and their excitements in the subsequent coaching sessions reflect their authenticity and sincerity. The executive is briefed by the coach about the purpose of undertaking this exercise.

Step 3: When the executive is ready for this exercise, the coach gives the executive the "Value Game" sheet, as given in Annexure 5.1. The executive is asked initially to identify top ten values from the lists. It is important here to ensure that the list is not very long and each item in the list is value, not motive, trait, or attitude.

Step 4: In the next coaching session, the coach facilitates the executive to identify the top five values from the ten values identified in the previous steps, by asking probing and clarifying question, and discarding those that are not truly reflecting his values.

Step 5: The coach then takes up the value clarification process with the executive. In the value clarification process, the coach facilitates the executive to examine their lives from the past experiences or life journey and share with the coach when the executive had honored or not honored that particular value and the consequences thereon. When the executive explores each value one by one from the list with the coach in a safe yet courageous environment, the executive moves back and forth in their life journey and tries to find the answer about themselves who they are.

Step 6: Finally, executive identifies the most important five values they have, by reflecting upon several high and low points of their life's journey, difficult and trying situations they have faced, and the happiest moments of their life. After identification of the top five values of the executive, the coach guides the executives to introspect themselves inside out to explore what these values mean to them and how they are going to honor them

- *Identification of developmental needs:* After clarifying the values, the executive with the assistance with the coach distills key insights from 360-degree feedback and other assessments they completed prior to this phase. This helps the executive refine their understanding of their leadership competencies, styles, and behaviors, which impact in their current role as well as future role inside the organization and other stakeholders. Based on the deeper conversation with the coach and self-reflection, the executive is able to identify their leadership developmental needs.

Finally, the coach develops a leadership development report that:

- Summarizes the leadership profile and style of the executive
- Articulates areas of strength to leverage against their leadership aspirations
- Develops opportunities to work on to support their leadership growth aspirations

- The next phase of leadership coaching is the identification of leadership growth areas. The executive articulates with his coach two or three priority areas of leadership growth which will impact his leadership effectiveness significantly. These two or three areas of leadership growth could be in the area of behavior change or leadership competency development or specific skill development, e.g., strategic planning or commercial acumen.

- *Goal setting:* After identifying the leadership growth areas, the next stage is to set the goal for each development area. It is important to understand here that the goals can create different understandings for different people. Some executives may think of a goal as achieving an ultimate objective, a behavior, or an action. For example, some executives may say we would like to reduce stress, want more top-line growth, would like to delegate more, have more team engagement, etc. However, no goal setting is complete, unless and until the executive is clear what is the ultimate value for them in achieving their goals. Hence, the challenge for leadership coach is to create enough opportunity for the executive to reflect on what these goals mean to them and what are the rewards and pleasures associated with achieving a goal. If the goals are aligned with their values, purpose, and vision of their life, then only the goals are meaningful for them, else there will be dissonance. Hence full exploration of each leadership goal by the executive with the help of coach is essential so that the executive can connect with their goals emotionally and can be much more motivated and excited to achieve their goals. As compared to other niche of corporate coaching, leadership coach helps the executive develop a deeper and a detailed vision of their future so that they can be in touch with purpose and meaning of their future, which ultimately lead to higher motivation and commitments in achieving their leadership goals.

- *Action planning:* Next, the leadership coach engages with the executive in the leadership development process by helping them develop a detailed action plan, assisting them in taking actions, discussing with them what are the organizational challenges and brainstorm with them how to overcome them, monitoring the progress of action plan, working as accountability partner in the process and for their success.

- *Coaching:* Leadership coach works with the executive while the executive starts taking actions as per plan, brainstorms with him the challenges and roadblocks, and supports the executive throughout the coaching journey by acknowledging, motivating, encouraging, and creating an environment of learning and growth.

Chapter Summary

Leadership coaching is for high achievers, who are quite effective in their roles but would like to enhance their leadership competencies or for those who are in transition to leadership role from managerial role or for those who are being groomed for leadership positions within the organization. Leadership coaching focuses both on transactional and on transformational issues of the executive/employee, besides encompassing areas such as the ability to develop trust and authenticity within the organization, ability to develop satisfactory relationship with board, shareholders, external world, ability to align executives/employees to the organization's vision and strategic objectives, and ability to lead from the front. Leadership coaching helps successful leaders understand themselves fully their own strengths, values, beliefs, and emotional quotient.

High-performing organizations undertake leadership coaching not only to enhance leadership competencies for a few selective leaders but also to create leadership pipeline aligning with the organizational leadership framework so that potential leaders are groomed appropriately to meet the strategic objectives of the organization in sustainable fashion.

Leadership coaching starts with creating a leadership map of the executives so that the executives get deeper insight of their life journey so far, defining moments in the organization, their inner strengths, their beliefs and values, their potential to grow, and aspirations so that they can decide the path they would like to take in the leadership journey. Finally the leadership coach works with the executive on enhancing leadership competencies as per the developmental need of the executive/employee.

Annexure 5.1: The Value Game

Circle below 10 Values That You Use in Life

(You may combine two or three values as long as critical distinctions are not lost. Example: Honesty/Integrity/Authenticity).

Acceptance	Enlightenment	Loyalty	Self-expression
Accomplishment	Excellence	Magnificence	Serenity
Accuracy	Faith	Mastery	Service
Altruism	Family	Nurture	Sincerity
Authenticity	Feeling	Orderliness	Spirit
Beauty	Forgiveness	Originality	Spirituality
Bravery	Freedom	Patience	Strength
Candor	Grace	Peacefulness	Superiority
Clarity	Guidance	Perfection	Tenderness
Commitment	Harmony	Personal growth	Thoughtfulness
Compassion	Health	Persuasion	Trust
Completion	Honesty	Pleasure	Truth
Conformity	Honor	Power	Understanding
Contentment	Imagination	Prosperity	Unity
Control	Influence	Quest	Vision
Courage	Information	Realization	Wholeness
Creativity	Inspiration	Recognition	Will
Dedication	Integration	Refinement	
Devotion	Integrity	Relationship	
Discernment	Intimacy	Religious	
Discovery	Invention	Responsibility	
Elegance	Justice	Reverence	
Empowerment	Learning	Satisfaction	
Encouragement	Love	Security	

Other values you consider important in your life:

....
....
....
....
....

Now select your five top values and define what each one means to you , by reflecting as to when you have used or stuck to that value in difficult or trying time or at cross-roads in your life journey. Write down the reasons for your choosing this value:

1. My most important value is ....,
   because ....
   ....

2. My next important value is ...., because
   ....
   ....

3. My next important value is ...., because
   ....
   ....

4. My next important value is ...., because
   ....
   ....

5. My next important value is ...., because
   ....
   ....

Discuss each value with your Coach in the next session. Before that, please go through this list couple of times and reflect deeply on your life journey so far and add, change or modify the reasons you have written or thoughts about against each value or add one or two values where you may be having confusion. You may like to discuss this value list with your close friends (whom you have long relationship) and ask their opinions or views.

References

Blanchard, K. (2005). The servant leader as coach. In H. Morgan, P. Harkins, & M. Goldsmith (eds), *The art and practice of leadership coaching*. Hoboken, New Jersey: John Wiley & Sons.

Cogner, J. (2005). Coaching leaders. In H. Morgan, P. Harkins, & M. Goldsmith (eds), *The art and practice of leadership coaching*. Hoboken, New Jersey: John Wiley & Sons.

Kouzes, J. (2005). Coaching for credibility. In H. Morgan, P. Harkins, & M. Goldsmith (eds), *The art and practice of leadership coaching*, pp. 80–82. Hoboken, New Jersey: John Wiley & Sons.

Mukherjee, S. (2011). Harnessing executive's values in coaching. *International Journal of Mentoring and Coaching*, XII, pp. 86–94.

Siegal, K. (2005). Coaching leaders/behavioural coaching. In H. Morgan, P. Harkins, & M. Goldsmith (eds), *The art and practice of leadership coaching*. Hoboken, New Jersey: John Wiley & Sons.

CHAPTER 6

Coaching for Talent Management

What Is Talent Management?

The Chartered Institute of Personnel and Development (CIPD) defines talent "as of those individuals, who can make a difference to organizational performance either through their immediate contribution or, in the longer term, by demonstrating the highest levels of potential." CIPD defines talent management as, "… the systematic attraction, identification, development, engagement, retention and deployment of those individuals who are of particular value to an organization, either in view of their 'high potential' for the future or because they are fulfilling business/operation-critical roles." According to American Society of Training and Development (ASTD), "Talent management is a holistic approach to optimizing human capital, which enables an organization to derive short and long-term results by building culture, engagement, capability and capacity through integrated talent acquisition, development and deployment processes that are aligned to business goals." There are four aspects of talent management. Hence, these are identifying, attracting, developing, and retaining talent.

Challenges in Talent Management Programs

Organizations are being forced by circumstances to have effective talent management programs to keep their talented employees within the organization and develop them for future leadership role. Attracting and retaining talent are immensely challenging issues for human resource department, since top talent is always in short supply. Conaty and Charan (2010) quote,

> Talent will be the big differentiator between companies that succeed and those that don't. Those companies that win will be led by people who can adapt their organizations to change, make the right strategic bets, take calculated risks, conceive and execute new value-creating opportunities, and build and rebuild competitive advantage.

Human resource function of every organization faces the problem of availability of a limited number of talented employees within organizations who could be groomed for leadership roles. Other challenges for human resource department are that organizations spend a lot of time and money in recruiting talents at the entry level of management. These new recruits undergo a structured and comprehensive development program for twelve to eighteen months (nowadays it is a few months to maximum one year). After these employees get inducted within an organization at different functions or roles after the induction program, they get lost in the crowd. There is actually no system to keep track on exploiting their potential in continual basis and keeping them engaged and motivated.

Even if organizations could retain some of their emerging talents for a longer period of time, there is no effective compensation management system to differentiate the reward structure for these groups of employees from others. Some of these talented employees are well aware of their privileged positions in the organization and they would like to take maximum benefits, financial and otherwise, from the organization. Hence, organizations are continuously reengineering their human resource policy so that the talent management program is kept in pace with that of the other organizations, so that retention of talent is possible.

It was observed during the last two decades that human resource function was more focused on attracting individuals with high potential in the organizations. In the area of attracting talent, organization focuses on creating an employer brand so that the potential employee would like to join the organization. Organizations are also putting their best efforts in selecting the right talent for the organization. Traditional recruitment processes and practices have undergone substantial changes. Organizations have, of late, started using psychometric tools in the selection process. Some organizations are also using competency-based selection, wherein assessment centers are being conducted to select candidates based on competency requirements of the organization.

But now, the focus of the organizations is shifted more toward developing, managing, and retaining talent as an important part of human resource management strategy in alignment with the overall business strategy. Organizations are of people; people make the difference in creating the values in the organization through business processes and systems. Rightly so, talent management has become one of the most important buzzwords in corporate human resource function.

Talent Management Process

Let us now briefly discuss the talent management process in an organization. It consists of the following broad steps:

Critical competencies analysis: Each organization requires a set of competencies to meet its business objectives. Hence each organization identifies key organizational competencies, which all its managerial resources must have, and a set of functional or role competencies, which are essential for the role holders to possess to perform their responsibilities. The first step in talent management process is to take stock of competencies. In this step, organization undertakes the following broad activities:

- Identify critical roles in the organization for the next five to ten years based on the strategic plan of the organization.
- Identify competencies required for the critical roles.
- Identify competency gaps, which are in urgent need and which are required in medium to long term.

Talent identification: After identifying critical competencies, it is important to identify how many employees are available within the organization to take up the future roles and responsibilities. To do that, large organizations have structured talent management schemes. In this scheme, organizations prepare a talent list once in a year or once in two years, based on the specific criteria of selection. Generally the selection criteria include qualification, experience, age, potential to grow, and performance during the last two to three years. Generally, departmental/functional leaders, besides other sectional managers, are involved in identification of emerging talents in their functional areas.

The role of functional leaders is to identify potential leaders from the existing manpower resources they have. It is not only their technical competencies and performance track records but their values, their workplace behavior, their ability to influence others, early leadership signs, extraordinary talent displayed, etc. These are some of the important areas the functional leaders look in preparation of the potential talent list. Some organizations prefer conducting interviews of each member of the potential talent list to ensure that the identified employees meet the criteria of talent selection. Each department or function generally identifies 10–15 percent of the total strength of the department, as potential talent. Finally, the human resource department in consultation with functional heads finalize the talent list for the organization.

Some organizations prefer that each employee undergoes structured assessment process before preparing a potential talent list for the organization. For that, assessment centre approach is deployed to assess the competencies of the executives against the organizational or role competencies. Based on the assessment center data, organization finalizes the talent list for the organization. Some organizations conduct 360-degree multi-rater assessment technique to evaluate the competency level of existing employees.

One challenge human resource department faces is whether to announce the talent list in public or keep it confidential. If the talent list is not announced or declared by the organization, then how the identified employee will know that they are in the talent list of the organization and the organization is going to put additional efforts in their development. Talent development cannot be done in secret within any organization. On the other hand, the high-performing employees, who are not in the potential talent list, may get demotivated and may like to leave the organization. Hence, proper articulation and company-wide communication of talent management scheme, i.e., the process of identification of talent as well as the growth prospect of the employees who are not in the talent list are undertaken by the human resource department.

Talent review: Talent review is a yearly exercise for most of the organizations, wherein the Chief Executive Officer (CEO) takes stock of the talent required vis-à-vis that available in the organization. Besides the CEO, all functional heads and Head HR are generally the members of talent review meeting. The agenda of talent review meeting are:

- To review business priorities with specific reference to key competencies required
- To review present and proposed organizational structures
- To anticipate vacancy at leadership levels due to expected separations for the coming one year
- To review talent on readiness to take up positions in short and medium time frame
- To review the development plan of each executive/employee in the talent list
- To decide on what actions to be taken where no internal talent is available

Talent attraction: In some situations, the organization may not have people with the required competencies or it may not be possible to develop the competencies internally. In such cases, the organization undertakes competency-based recruitment system to induct talent from outside. However, attracting talent is a very difficult process for any organization broadly for two reasons. First, the availability of talent in the marketplace is limited, for which the organization puts efforts in building the best employer brand in the marketplace and creates conducive employment conditions in the organization so that new employees get integrated with the organizational culture and systems. Second, when talent is inducted from outside, new employees bring with them their value sets and cultural ethos, which sometimes may not be aligned with the existing organizational culture and ethos. Hence, inducting new employees (including experienced professional) and integrating them with the organizational processes and systems is an important task for the human resource department. After recruiting talent from outside, the human resource department also identifies the developmental needs of these employees and how to integrate these employees with the existing talent development program of the organization.

Talent development: Development of talent is a continuous process. Talent review meeting finalizes the developmental plan for each employee in the talent list. The developmental plan may include on-the-job training, training for new skills, sponsoring for development programs conducting internally or externally, self-learning, working with a mentor for acquiring hard skill, working with a coach for enhancement of soft skill, or behavior change or improvement of performance, job rotation, job enhancement, involvement in special taskforce or assignment, deputation to other function or department for short period, etc. The following are major talent developmental strategies:

1. *Training program*
Training programs are the most common method used by organizations in talent development for enhancement of skills, abilities,

and knowledge. Normally, employers sponsor employees to attend external or internal training programs. These programs provide the employees an opportunity for reflection during group problem-solving sessions and learning from others. The training programs also provide them with opportunities to hear how people from other professions, departments, or organizations approach certain situations. Such experiences and the training itself help employees to face and deal with real organizational problems.

2. Reading and sharing

Another strategy for the development of talent is encouraging employees to read books related to the particular subject or self-help books or watching management development videos or related movie clips from YouTube (www.Youtube.com). Employees may be asked to prepare a summary of the book or video, key learning points, and the ideas that can be implemented at the personal level or at workplace. This summary can be shared with peers by making presentations in the organization. The concept of study circle can also be implemented by organizations, wherein the employees are encouraged to share their learning. They are encouraged to present the summary of books read or to organize discussions. These study circles are informal groups of 20–30 employees, which voluntarily meet every week or fortnight for one to two hours.

3. Mentoring under an expert

Traditionally, training programs are very generic and cover the needs of wide-ranging participants, whereas mentoring programs allow a flexible, adaptive, and individual-centric skill development environment. Mentoring is a one-to-one activity, focusing purely on acquiring new skills or getting new work-related knowledge by facilitative support of the mentor. If a particular skill needs to be developed, then the executive is assigned a mentor, who is a known expert in that skill. The executive is advised to observe his mentor's actions or talk to him for advice and/or meet him at regular intervals to discuss his/her developmental needs and draw a plan of action. The mentor facilitates the employee to implement his/her developmental action plans to improve skill under his mentorship.

4. *Job rotation or membership in cross-functional team*
Job rotation is a very potent approach for developing specific competencies within employees through hands-on experience. In a very rare and genuine circumstance, when someone cannot be spared from an existing assignment for job rotation, nominating the executive for a project team or cross-functional team (CFT) could be considered. Essentially, CFTs provide the employee a multi-disciplinary perspective of problems that overlap in terms of department boundaries. Participating in a CFT and/or working on a special project team could be a useful option to get hands-on exposure to new fields.

5. *Job enrichment/job enlargement*
Existing jobs may hold tremendous potential for development, depending on their challenges. This may be done by adding challenging activities to the current job in order to promote development of a particular skill. Job enlargement, which is providing additional responsibility to what is currently handled, could be an option with the aim of development of the individual.

6. *Coaching*
Coaching is a one-to-one process in which the coach encourages the commitment of the employee to enhance performance and promote a climate of motivation. The coach–buddy relationship is one of mutual trust where the coach helps the employee discover himself. The focus is on helping the employee prepare an action plan for improvement of a few chosen crucial behaviors or skills or to tackle performance issues. Coaching is advisable when the executive meets the threshold levels of knowledge and skills but needs strengthening on one or two competencies or of some behaviors that may be most important for his growth.

Coaching Process for Talent Development

Briefly the coaching for talent development follows the following processes, which are customized based on the specific organizational requirements:

1. Normally, organizations will have an individual talent development plan for identified talents. Not all of them need coaching intervention. Hence, the first step is to identify the employees need coaching and what are the expectations from the coaching intervention. Sometimes, individual employees may need mentoring for acquiring specific job-related skills, but coaching has been recommended instead of mentoring.

2. The human resource department then identifies a pool of external coaches for talent development. Generally, most of the employees in the talent list are at the middle level of management or front line managers having leadership potential. Hence, the external coaches should be able to address both the transactional and transformational agenda of the employees. Many times, the organization hires C-level coaches for talent management program at very high cost, which may not be appropriate for these levels of executives. Some organizations prefer to have internal coaches, generally from the human resource department, to optimize cost but these internal coaches are not appropriately trained on coaching skills and have limited diversified organizational experiences. Hence, selection of coaches is an important step in talent management programs.

3. Each coach brings with them specific expertise, domain knowledge, experience, and coaching approach. Hence, it is advisable that the employee and coach matching is done based on the developmental needs of the executive. For example, one employee may need coaching on marketing planning area, the other employee may require coaching in improving his interpersonal skills, some employees may

need coaching on commercial acumen or customer handling skill, and so on. Hence, selection of the coach will depend on whether the coach has familiarity or some experience in dealing with such issues.

4. Coaching for talent development is focused on specific developmental needs identified by the management. Hence, the coach will focus on only one or two developmental needs that require coaching intervention. It is therefore different than executive coaching, where assessment is done by the coach to identify the coaching agenda. The role of the coach is first to understand from the management on what are the expectations on the deliverable of the coaching, timeline, monitoring mechanism, evaluation process, and role of management. The management also shares with the coach the details of the employee, which include his strengths, areas of development, performance records, experiences, etc.

5. The coach then meets with the employees to understand from them what are their work challenges, their background, their journey so far, who are their peers, customers (internal and external), suppliers as well as their career aspiration.

6. After developing an initial rapport with the executive, the coach helps the executive to develop developmental goals for the identified areas of development and facilitates the process of goal setting and action planning. For action planning, the GROW model of performance coaching can be effectively used with the executive/employee, so that the executive/employee can develop an action plan in a systematic manner. The coach then helps the executives/employees to achieve their goals following the process of executive coaching as mentioned in the previous chapter.

Talent retention: Finally, retention of talent is the most critical component in talent management program of any organization. Organization spends millions of dollars in development of talent pool of the organization, but if such executives/employees are not retained with the organization, then the total investment goes as a waste. Organizations hence implement a structured development process for the potential talents as well as reward them differently from the rest of the executives/employees, based on the unique contribution made by these executives/employees and specific skill-sets they possess. This ultimately helps the organization for long-term benefits, by retaining these executives/employees.

Chapter Summary

In the twenty-first century, organizations are facing greater complexities and challenges in the area of talent management. The conventional and well-established skill-building or capability-building techniques used in talent management are not sufficient. After inducting talent in the organization, there exists different ways of grooming fresh talent or new incumbents into organizations. There are mainly four areas of talent management: attracting talent, developing talent, managing talent, and finally retaining talent. Organizations first identify critical competencies required among its key human resources to meet the strategic objectives of the organization as well as to maintain its competitive advantages. Based on the skills and competencies required in the short and medium terms, organization conducts annual talent review process to identify what talents are available within their organization or could be developed by the organization and what are the resources to be recruited. Development of talent is a continuous process. Organization first develops an individual talent developmental plan for identified talents, so that the available talents are ready to meet the organizational requirements in short to medium terms. Since each talented executive/employee has a specific developmental need, coaching has become one of the powerful and effective tools in the development of talents within the organization. Coaches work with individual executive/employee to ensure that each talent works with his/her own developmental plan, as decided by the organization. The coach assists the executive/employee to define developmental goals, decide the strategies to meet the developmental goals, and finally help them frame action plans to achieve the goals. The coach facilitates the executives/employees to achieve their development goals by keeping them focused on the developmental agenda and arranges necessary organization resources and supports so that the talent management program objectives are achieved.

Reference

Conaty, B. & Charan, R. (2010). *The talent masters: Why smart leaders put people before numbers*. London: Random House Business Books.

CHAPTER 7

Internal Coaching

Developing Internal Coaching Capabilities

What Does Internal Coaching Mean?

Executive coaching is increasingly used as a strategy for developing human capital within the organization. According to the Hay Group study, 25–40 percent of Fortune 500 companies used executive coaches for increasing performance, employee satisfaction, and business results. However, in difficult economic climates, the organizations face budgetary constraints to implement large-scale executive coaching interventions to address urgent needs of developing a large number of executives to face organizational challenges. The emerging trend in executive coaching is, therefore, on developing a pool of coaches within the organization from the existing resources, either from human resource function or from the other functional areas and from those working at leadership positions, who can take additional responsibility of coaching one or more executives in the same organization. This is known as Internal Coaching in coaching domain. Frisch (2001) offers the following definition of internal coaching:

> Internal Coaching is a one-on-one departmental intervention supported by the organization and provided by a colleague of those coached who is trusted to shape and deliver a program yielding individual professional growth.

Why Internal Coaching?

In many organizations the responsibility of employee development shifted from the human resource department to line managers over a period of time. The role of the human resource department is now shifted from taking ownership of employee development to facilitating the process. The reason behind such a shift is that it is not possible for the human resource department alone to undertake development agenda of a large number of executives/employees within the organization. Therefore, organizations have started using the services of line managers, who have better executive/employee development skills and are interested in developing their subordinates, in employee development and skill-building efforts.

Internal coaching is deployed within the organizations for various purposes. The major purpose for organizations is to impart coaching for a large number of executives/employees in a shorter period of time. Such organizations believe that when senior managers and leaders are trained for coaching skills and they impart coaching to other executives/employees (mostly junior to them), a coaching culture slowly develops within the organization.

The quality of leadership is widely accepted as critical in the success of a business enterprise. Organizations rise and fall on how effectively they use their human resources. Many organizations use internal coaching intervention to develop leadership pipeline within the organization. These organizations train managers and leaders, who would be imparting internal coaching, to develop their coaching skills and competencies, so that they can provide internal coaching to other employees with confidence. For example, Lockheed Martin, a Fortune 100 company, developed an extensive internal coach certification program so that the certified coaches could optimally support executives in high-potential executive development program. When Lockheed Martin turned to the question of how to best grow and strengthen its leaders within its leadership models and organizational commitments, the important strategic direction for the organization was to establish an internal coach certification program. Oil and National Gas Corporation, a *navaratna* public sector undertaking in oil and gas exploration business in India, introduced an internal coaching certification program for senior managers to develop internal coaching capabilities so that the large number of potential leaders and high-performing managers can be coached for preparing them to take leadership positions in medium- to long-term time horizon.

In internal coaching, when the coach is a leader, coaching other executive/employees in the organization has a dual advantage. Here, not only the person being coached benefits from the relationship but also the leader, who is coaching, gets several direct and indirect benefits from the coaching experience. Moreover, the development of internal coaching capabilities in sustainable ways helps the organization to address the cost pressure.

Internal Coaching for Coaching Culture Building

Organizations are facing two major challenges in people front. It is becoming difficult to induct right talent at the leadership level. On the other hand, retention of talent for longer term within the organization, mostly at the middle level, is another challenge. It is not very uncommon to find that high-performing managers in an organization have made rapid progress in their early career due to their strong technical competencies or financial acumen, but hit the corporate ceiling due to the lack of right skill sets, so essential once they go up the corporate ladder. It is a standard trend in the industry to promote people who have excellent technical expertise. These new managers suddenly find themselves in a position where they have to manage subordinates, "believe in them," "encourage them," "share with them," and "trust them." They are assigned the added responsibility of developing their subordinates, besides looking after productivity, morale, and job satisfaction, with no guidance on how to coach them. They are expected to contribute in developing a "Learning Culture" in the organization. These new managers continue to mentor subordinates on their technical skills rather than leading, encouraging, and appreciating them. The result is dissatisfied and de-motivated subordinates who quit at the first available opportunity.

The skills required at higher levels of management range from the ability to handle interpersonal relationships, the ability to manage a team, how to delegate, or manage change. When a technical manager undergoes a transition to a significantly more senior role, where the role requires different competencies, they need to learn new ways of working and add new skills with regard to the ability to handle interpersonal relationships, ability to manage team, strategic planning, change management, etc. Coaching helps these managers acquire new skills and competencies, so that they can effectively manage their team members and allow the potential leaders to grow under them. It is important for the mangers at a higher level of management to move from "command and control" style of managing to "supporting and facilitating" role. Moreover, the following values and behaviors need to be displayed by managers, who reached to senior management positions:

1. Showing respect for the person   vs. "I'm the boss"
2. Asking and inquiring   vs. "Telling and directing"
3. Exploring at a deeper level with curiosity   vs. Being judgmental
4. Displaying personal integrity   vs. Do as I say, not as I do
5. Giving and receiving feedback   vs. Being pretentious
6. Encouraging growth and learning   vs. Penalizing for failures
7. Partnering and collaborating   vs. "I'm the expert"
8. Solution-focused   vs. Problem-focused
9. Empowering and guiding   vs. Managing and controlling
10. Giving constructive feedback   vs. Criticizing and invalidating

However, when a large number of managers and leaders in organizations display the opposite behaviors, a culture of mediocrity within the organization is created along with low motivation levels amongst a large percentage of executives/employees. This is partly because of the perceived time constraints of the managers and the pressure of delivering bottom-line results. The perceived role of a solution provider by many of these managers contributes to why they prefer to just tell and direct rather than ask and inquire. To promote a coaching culture within organizations, the managers need to use more of an inquiry and questioning approach to help their subordinates learn to think for themselves rather than a telling and directing approach. One of the main functions of a manager is to influence their subordinates for the achievement of work objectives. These managers, in influencing roles, not only solve problems and help their subordinates, but also have an impact on others' ability to solve future problems. They are also responsible for the growth of their subordinates, instead of making them dependent on them.

It is, therefore, strongly recommended that organizations should start realizing that investing resources in developing internal coaching is far more beneficial for the organization than any other development initiatives, since there is a long-term benefit of the enhanced capability of their managers, which in turn helps organizations in building skills on a continual basis rather than one of activity.

External Executive Coaching vis-à-vis Internal Executive Coaching

Generally, organizations prefer to hire external coaches to drive efforts toward building a coaching culture. Hiring external coaches for a large number of executives/employees and deploying them in large numbers for longer period is not an easy task. Besides cost factors, building the coaching culture within the organization requires the involvement of a high percentage of executives/employees in the change effort. Organization needs to weigh the benefits and costs of hiring external coaches against developing their own cadre of internal coaches or using some combination of internal and external resources. One of the obvious benefits of internal coaching is that it is far less expensive than hiring external coaches. The second advantage of internal coaching is the coaching initiative is not necessarily restricted to a few executives at senior levels but a large number of executives in the middle-management level get involved in the coaching intervention. Internal coaches, generally, have the advantage of understanding the organization's business issues and internal dynamics. The internal coaches are aware of the executive's context and they speak the language of the organization. Since internal coaches are part of the organization, they are easily accessible to the executives and they are available whenever the need arises. Internal coaches, sometimes, go out of the way to organize resources or get support from their colleagues, if their executives have a specific need that is not available with the coach. Internal coaches are also much aware of what are possible and not possible, what resources are available, or could be organized within the organization. Hence, they can develop pragmatic but practical developmental plans as compared to external coaches. If the internal coaches are successful managers in leadership positions, then the coaches may find it easier to gain respect of the executives and build rapport, as compared to external coaches. In internal coaching, when the coach is a manager, senior manager, or leader, coaching other executives/employees in the organization has a dual advantage. Here, not only the person being coached but also the internal coach who is coaching benefits from the relationship. Teaching managers to coach is not only cost-effective for sustainable long-term organizational benefits, but there are great benefits to internal coaches in terms of their personal and professional gains.

In general, the internal coaches have less coaching and cross-organizational experience compared to the external coaches. Internal coaches usually have less experience in coaching, since they have a fewer opportunities to hone their coaching skills. Owing to their lack of cross-organization exposure, they may have limited understanding on the whole gamut of executive coaching skills, experiences, and opportunities. The issue of confidentiality is a concern with internal coaching as compared to external coaching, since the internal coaches are not generally very senior managers and they have much more interaction with other members of the organization than that of external coaches. The credibility of external coaches is generally higher than that of internal coaches in the executives' mind; hence, trust and confidentiality are perceived more by the executives with the external coaches. Hence, the internal coaches take additional care in maintaining confidentiality of their executives to ensure their own credibility as a coach. Finally, internal coaches have other responsibilities within the organization, which may sometimes affect the coaching outcomes, whereas the external coaches have only one responsibility, i.e., coaching in the organization.

Some organizations prefer hiring external executive coaches for executives at very senior levels of the organization and internal coaching is limited to middle levels of the management only. However, whether to have external coaches or internal coaches or both depends on the following criteria:

1. Level of executives/employees under coaching intervention
2. Cost of coaching
3. Duration of coaching
4. Nature of interventions, i.e., primarily on transactional or transformational issues for coaching
5. Availability of right coaches, with required skills and related experience in coaching in similar context
6. In-depth understanding of business and the industry

Implementation of Internal Coaching Program

Within an organizational context, coaching is often discussed in the same vein as mentoring, because coaching and mentoring share common elements (Smith et al., 2009). Hence, before implementing an internal coaching program, it is important to understand "what" of internal coaching, i.e., what are the goals of the interventions, what it is, and what it is not. Internal coaching program only becomes effective if it is clearly defined, the process is standardized, and it is articulated well throughout the organization.

Cross and Lynch (1988) put forward "The Smart Performance Pyramid" model, which integrates performance through hierarchy of the organization. Leedham (2005) adopted this model for coaching context, as the Coaching Benefits Pyramid Model. The model is based on the principle that in order to be fully effective, a coaching relationship (which includes internal coaching) must be built on four key factors:

1. The skills of the coach (listening, questioning, giving clear feedback, establishing rapport, and providing support)
2. The personal attributes of the coach (knowledge, experience, qualifications, ability to inspire, and belief in the executive's potential)
3. The coaching process (clearly structured and disciplined, providing mental challenge, and growth opportunities for the executive)
4. The coaching environment (a safe, supportive place to discuss confidential and sensitive issues, providing time and space for the executive to think and reflect)

Skills of the coach: To develop the necessary coaching skills within the potential internal coach managers, it is important the coaching skill program is designed carefully so that the skills components of the program are covered in-depth. It is important here to note that "Coaching for Manager" is not sufficient enough for development of internal coaches. Generic program on "Coaching for Manager" is primarily focused on creating awareness of the role of coaching in managing and leading executive/employee, so that the manager may use coaching besides mentoring, leading, and managing their subordinates. However, "Internal Coaching Skill" training is designed to impart basic coaching skills to potential internal coaches, so that they can effectively deploy the coaching skills while imparting coaching to their executives.

The internal coach skill training program is generally designed and conducted by a senior executive coach, generally external coach, so that the participants of the program get familiarized with the challenges the coaches face during coaching, the issues to be confronted while imparting coaching, as well as how to handle difficult coaching situations. Coaching is a skill-based intervention. Hence short two- or three-day coaching skill training is not sufficient for imparting necessary skills to the internal coaches. Learning to coach is like learning to drive. After initial training, these coaches are supported with additional inputs and additional skills to refine their existing skills as they practice their skills in real-time coaching. Input on communication skills, interpersonal skills, feedback skills, and understanding executive/employee's transactional and managerial styles is also included in the internal coach skill training program.

The coach: Some organizations prefer to develop internal coaches from the existing human resource professionals, which include L&D, OD professional, because of their inherent strengths of in-depth understanding of the organizational priorities in terms of developmental agenda of the organization, and they are trained on specialized skills of people management. However, the coaching skills are quite different from people management skills, interpersonal skills, or leadership training. Majority of human resource professionals are from operational HR role or working in L&D function as trainers on a specialized domain or doing administrative functions. It is important to identify successful managers, including human resource managers, who have high credibility within the organization for their performance, their leadership capability, their level of commitment in developing their second line, and their interest in development of their team members. Though the qualification, training, and professional background of the managers of the potential internal coach are not important, it is important that they are working at senior managerial levels in the organization. Therefore, the selection of potential coaches is to be based on their personal attributes, their people management skills, their past achievements, their credibility within the organization as well as their willingness to get involved in the process. However, when human resource professionals are trained as internal coach, the skills of HR professionals are enhanced, which results in more effective role of these professionals in the development process of the organization. Hence, selection of managers as internal coaches is a very important component for effective coaching intervention.

Frisch (2001) suggests twelve competencies that an effective internal coach should

- Build trusting relationship
- Understand and execute the specified coaching model
- Possess psychological curiosity
- Articulate observations in simple and useful terminology
- Understand how executives/employees develop and change over times
- Have an innovative and creative approach to their work
- Have expertise in management issues
- Have good listening skills
- Balance commitment both to executives/employees and to the organization
- Be open to continuous learning opportunities
- Seek and accept help when issues arise that are beyond their expertise
- Gain satisfaction from helping executives/employees and seeing the organization develop

The coaching process: Each organization has its own objectives to initiate internal coaching interventions. It could be for developing leadership pipeline or improving and imparting soft skills for selected executive/employees on continual basis or supporting managers in transitions or on-boarding of new executives/employees or using for the talent management process. Hence, the organization identifies a specific coaching model that will be effective for them to achieve the internal coaching objectives and goals. The coaching model helps the organization define clearly the coaching process to be followed. The Delta Coaching Model discussed in Chapter 2 of this book is one such example.

Another important part of the coaching process is matching of executives with the coaches. It is a normal practice in internal coaching that the internal coaches do not take up coaching of their subordinates, i.e., the coach should not be the reporting officer, directly or indirectly, of the executives. In large organizations, it is possible to match the coaches with the executives, who have not worked with them directly, are not from the same functional domain, and the executives are at least one step lower in the hierarchy than that of the internal coach.

The next step is deciding the duration of each coaching session, the total number of coaching sessions, how the coaching agenda is to be fixed, what data, viz., performance data, engagement data, etc., will be made available to internal coaches, how the effectiveness of coaching will be monitored, etc. Compared to external executive coaching, internal coaches generally have one or two executives and the duration of coaching is around six months, whereas the external coaches are generally engaged for nine months to twenty-four months.

The coaching environment: Before implementing internal coaching in the organization, the following factors are to be considered in creating the right coaching environment:

- The perceptions and expectations of all stakeholders in the organization, which include the business leaders, human resources, functional heads, and executives/employees in general, for the interventions are to be understood and defined.

- Sometimes there is skepticism or negative story with coaching or coaching initiatives undertaken earlier. If yes, appropriate strategy is to be framed to address the issues upfront before starting the process.

- How continuous feedbacks from all the stakeholders are to be collected to increase the effectiveness of the program.

The internal coaches are expected to focus on the changing mindset of managing, directing to one of helping and facilitating their executive for self-learning and self-awareness. One of the critical parameters of success of any internal coaching is the trust level between the internal coach and the executive/employee. Trust is a delicate flower, it can flourish only when the coach can create the right environment by displaying a high level of integrity, honesty, openness, fairness, and respect. The coach, therefore, ensures that the coaching is conducted in an environment where the executive feels comfortable to share and discuss with the coach on their challenges and get motivated to a learning process. It is advisable that the coaching is conducted not in the office of the internal coach during normal working hours, but to identify a relaxing and comfortable place where the coach and the executive can discuss without any distractions.

Case Example

Oil and Natural Gas Corporation limited is the largest oil and gas exploration public sector company in India, ranked 357 in Fortune 500 companies. ONGC had embarked upon an internal coaching initiative during 2008–2010. The objectives of the coaching initiative as identified by ONGC were as follows:

- To develop an internal coaching program, which will be custom designed by an independent agency (external executive coaching firm) to meet ONGC's needs and goals, keeping in view the organizational culture, the specific nature of its business, and diverse working conditions.
- To train the internal team members (Executive Director, Senior General Managers and General Managers) as internal coach to ensure long-term continuity in coaching initiative and development of in-house competency.

Contd.

Contd.

The role of internal coaches was defined by the organization in consultation with the external executive coaching firm as follows:

1. ONGC Internal Coaches will give the middle-managers (senior managers and deputy general managers) a clear understanding of their leadership behavior, style and impact; focuses on their core strengths, limitations, and developmental needs.
2. These coaches will help in identifying challenges in the executives "current and emerging roles and explores possible gaps between their skills and those challenges."
3. They will facilitate the executives' to focus on their developments over the next few months to increase their effectiveness.
4. They will handhold the executives in developing self-development plans, assist them in implementation of development plans, and translating them into new behavior at the workplace.

To develop internal coach, ONGC identified 45 leaders for this initiative. The author of this book was the project leader of this initiative on behalf of the external coaching firm. The brief process followed is given below:

- All identified leaders underwent three-day Internal Coaching Development Workshop. During the three-day workshops, the workshop leader explained the concept of coaching to the participants, focusing on the history of coaching, difference between Coaching, Consulting, Mentoring, Counseling, and Therapy, role of leaders as internal coach, etc. The participants were explained the coaching process through simulated coaching practice sessions and self-awareness through assessments. The participants also underwent extensive sessions on the skills of power listening, asking powerful questions and providing feedback during coaching sessions. Program design is given in Annexure 7.1.
- The coaches were given a Coach Diary and three Coachee Diaries each on the final day of the Coaching Skill Workshop to record the details of the coaching sessions and to guide them during their sessions.
- Coaching manual for the Coaches and Coachees was prepared explaining the coaching model, process, what are expected from them as coach/executive, and possible challenges of the process. These manuals were handed over to all participants at the end of the workshop.

Contd.

Contd.

- The coaches were provided with coaching tools and instruments to use during the coaching sessions to assist them in the coaching process. Some of the tools given to them were: The Wheel of Life, Visioning Exercise, set of Powerful Questions, GROW model of Performance Coaching, SPIRO-M Instrument, etc.
- The coaches were briefed on the ONGC coaching process and the accreditation process. At the end of the workshop, the coaches were asked to select 3 executives (coachees) each from their locations of work. The coaches were advised not to select executives from their own discipline and subordinates working under them. It was suggested that those who are identified as good performers are to be considered as executives. The coaches, who were unable to select executives on their own, were assigned coachees by the HR department. It has been observed that the coaching process started very fast and the effectiveness of coaching was very high, where the coaches selected the executives on their own after discussion with their peers and reporting officers.
- During the coaching journey, the coaches were in contact with Project Leader (external coach) regularly to get guidance, share their experiences, clarify the process, and also get more additional resources. Accordingly, the external coach handheld the trained internal coaches during the coaching journey and provided some of them with articles and videos on coaching. Their queries were resolved through phone calls and emails.
- The coaches were given guidelines on how to embark on their coaching journey. Some of the guidelines given to them include:

i. Before the First Session

1. Before the first session, go through the material provided in this diary.
2. Meet your executive and the executive's manager.
3. Give the Coachee's Diary to the executive.
4. Ask the executive to go through the material contained in his/her diary and fill up the forms as mentioned. Ask him/her to send the completed Information forms back to you at least one day before the first session.
5. Fix the date, time, and place for the first session. Always ensure the executive's convenience before setting a date. Ideally, the session should be fixed in the first half of the day, as both you and your executive will be fresh at this time of the day.

Contd.

Contd.

6. Sessions should be face-to-face and of minimum 60 minutes each.
7. You should determine the date of session based on both yours and the executive's convenience.

ii. During the First Session

1. Ensure that the coaching environment is private, comfortable, and undisturbed by external interruptions.
2. Have your coaching diary handy, and allow a moment or two before the scheduled time to get centered and review how you are going to run and manage the session.
3. Make every attempt to be available on time for every session. However, if you are getting delayed or need to cancel any session, inform the executive well in advance and fix the date and time for the next session.
4. During the first session, go through the forms filled by the executive and discuss each point one by one with him/her.
5. Discuss and try to understand your coachee's challenges at his/her workplace in terms of his/her:

   - Performance
   - Dealing with peers
   - Interpersonal issues
   - Managing performance of subordinates
   - Meeting expectations of reporting manager, etc.

iii. The Second Session

1. Between the first and second sessions, it is a good idea to spend 15–20 minutes talking to the executive's manager to understand:

   - Areas the executive is good at
   - Areas of improvement
   - Performance issues affecting his/her performance.

2. Also conduct a personal SWOT Analysis (Strengths, Weaknesses, Opportunities, and Threats) for the executive in this session. This will help him/her to identify:

   - Strengths in current job competencies
   - Areas of competence/knowledge that are weak and need development

Contd.

Contd.

> • Opportunities for future career aspirations and
> • Identify any threats that may prevent achieving these
> 3. Sessions 1 and 2 are discovery sessions. By the end of the discovery sessions, the executive should identify the following, with the coach's help:
>   • 1–2 areas to work on for the next 3–4 months
>   • Develop goals for the action areas, measure, and time plans to achieve them.
>
> ## iv. Subsequent Sessions
>
> 1. Once the areas of improvement and goals are identified, your prime task is to help the executive develop new or improved capabilities/ competencies. These could be the skills, knowledge, and attitudes executives need, to reach their important career and life goals.
> 2. Spend time during subsequent sessions in reviewing the action points of the previous sessions.
> 3. Also spend the first few minutes of each session discussing major events that have taken place since the last session, successes, and setbacks, if any.
> 4. Continue discussing on specific goals/action areas identified.
> 5. Conclude the session and review the action points for coaching.

Chapter Summary

Development of subordinates is emerging as a major role for managers in order to transform the work environment as a learning environment, wherein the employees are supported by their superiors in self-learning. In large organizations, where attracting and retaining scarce talent at middle management level is becoming difficult, there is emerging need to groom talent internally for developing leadership pipeline within the organization. Executive coaching is one of the approaches in developing competencies for emerging talent and managerial resources in transition. Since executive coaching intervention is very costly, the internal coaching in combination with executive coaching is now an emerging trend in corporate coaching domain. In internal coaching, the coach is a fellow employee of the same organization as the executive.

For development of internal coaching capability within organization, the selection of managers to be trained as potential coach is an important parameter for the success of the program. There is an advantage for human resource professional to take up the internal coaching role, but other successful managers having strong people developmental orientation and having high credibility within the organizations are also to be included in the program. Since coaching is a skill and quite different from mentoring or teaching, the coach training focuses on skill building and reinforcement of additional skills as managers practice coaching. Trust and confidentiality are important concerns in internal coaching; hence, the coaching process and coaching environment are critical components in the effective delivery of internal coaching within an organization.

In large organizations, when leaders are engaged in coaching their managers, a coaching capability is slowly built into the organization through cascading effects. The fact is, internal coaching is not only highly cost-effective, but the organizations derive significant sustainable benefits when the internal coaching process is deployed for the development of competencies in potential leaders. However, internal coaching will not be deployed in all coaching opportunities, especially considering organizational complexity, confidentiality, and other factors; it is a robust offshoot of executive coaching world and becoming popular in corporate coaching.

Annexure 7.1: Program Design of Internal Coach Development Workshop

Duration: Three days

DAY 1

1st Half
- What is coaching?
- History of coaching
- Difference between coaching, consulting, mentoring, counseling, and therapy
- Coaching in organizations
- Role of manager as an internal coach

2nd Half
- Coaching process
- Self-awareness through assessment of managerial styles (SPIRO-M)
- The wheel of life
- Coaching practice session on the wheel of life

DAY 2

1st Half
- Coaching for performance
- GROW model of performance coaching
- Coaching practice session on GROW model.
- The characteristics of powerful questions
- Using questions

2nd Half
- How to ask questions
- Powerful questions
- Coaching practice session on questions

DAY 3

1st Half
- Effective listening, active listening, power listening
- Role plays on listening
- Practice session on effective listening
- Effective feedback
- Importance of feedback in coaching
- How and when to give feedback
- Difference between coaching feedback and performance feedback

2nd Half
- Coaching skills practice sessions
- Psychometric tools in coaching
- Integration and review of coaching skills
- Internal coaching program, evaluation, accreditation
- Feedback and closing

References

Cross, K.F. & Lynch, R.L. (1988). The SMART way to sustain and define success. *National Productivity Review*, 8 (1), pp. 23–33.

Frisch, M. (2001). The emerging role of the executive coach. *Consulting Psychology Journal: Research and Practice*, 53 (4), pp. 24–25.

Leedham, M. (2005). The coaching scorecard: A holistic approach to evaluating the benefits of business coaching. *International Journal of Evidence Based Coaching and Mentoring*, 3 (2), pp. 30–44.

Smith, M.L., Oosten, E.B.V., & Boyatzis, R.E. (2009). Coaching for desired change. *Research in Organizational Change and Development*, 17, pp. 145–173.

CHAPTER 8

Corporate Coaching Power Tools

Corporate coaches use various coaching tools during the coaching process, whether it is performance coaching, behavioral coaching, executive coaching, or internal coaching. Some of the coaching tools are briefly referred in previous chapters. Effective use of coaching tool is an art that each coach masters over a period of time. This chapter covers some of the basic coaching tools that are commonly used by the coaches in any coaching engagement. The objective of this chapter is to provide an overview of some of the important coaching tools, so that these tools become a part of the coaching toolkit for corporate coaches. The basic coaching tools discussed in this chapter are power listening, reframing perspectives, powerful questioning, feedback, mirroring, and paraphrasing.

Listening

The best way to understand people is to listen to them. (Ralph Nichols)

Listening is an essential skill for managers but a very few in organizations have mastered this skill. It is not uncommon in organization to notice that managers are mostly used to talking and telling to their subordinates at workplace, rather than listening and learning. This is because they have strong belief of command and control style of managing, and their management style is directive. Listening is so important in organizations that it has been called by some as a primary skill in managing, leading, and problem-solving. By listening to subordinates in the workplace, the manager is saying, "I am not going to take over your problem. I believe you are capable of solving it." When the manager succeeds in communicating these messages through skillful listening, the employees are often willing to examine the issues more openly. The manager through listening conveys he cares about what the employee thinks and feels.

Most of us think that we listen, yet we do not always attend to the person speaking to us. We are too busy doing other things, or thinking about things, while someone is speaking to us. Sometimes, even we are composing reply in our head, i.e., how we will reply to them, while the other person is speaking to us, not hearing what actually is being said to us. Hearing and listening are not the same thing.

These are some important facts regarding listening:

- We listen at 125–250 words per minute, but think at 1,000–3,000 words per minute.
- That 85 percent of what we know, we have learned through listening.
- We usually recall only 50 percent of what we have heard immediately after listening to someone talk.
- We allow five seconds to our discussion partner to answer to our question.

We may be born with the ability to listen, but listening effectively is a skill that must be mastered. Whether you are a corporate coach or a manager coaching your team member, it is much more important to develop skill of listening. The essence of listening is being able to focus on what another person is saying without being distracted. When someone speaks, they want to feel heard; this need is ingrained in all of us. When we feel that we're not being listened to, it affects that most basic part of ourselves—our self-esteem.

Hearing is the first stage of listening. Hearing is the physiological process in which our ears pick up sound waves, which are then transported to our brain. Listening, on the other hand, is an active process that constructs meaning to it. There are six stages of the listening process:

1. *Hearing*: It refers to the responses caused by sound waves stimulating the sensory receptors of the ear.
2. *Attention*: Our brain screens stimuli and permits only a select few to come into focus. These selective perceptions are known as attention.
3. *Understanding*: The listener analyzes the meaning of the stimuli to understand the intended meaning and the context assumed by the sender.
4. *Remembering*: It means that an individual has not only received and interpreted a message but has also added it to his memory.
5. *Evaluating*: It is a stage in which the listener weighs evidence, sorts out facts from opinions, and determines the presence or absence of bias or prejudice in a message.
6. *Responding*: In this stage, the listener completes the process through verbal and/or nonverbal feedback.

Listening is not simply passive hearing. Listening involves more than what the executive client is speaking. Not only the coach hears the words the executive is speaking but also the tone, the pace, the body posture, expression, and the feelings being expressed. When a coach listens to his executive client, the coach also notices the energy level of the executive, i.e., whether it is low, flat, fluctuating, high, or sparking. The coach notices all that is coming to him in the form of information. Then the coach chooses when and what to respond and how to respond. The coach then notices the impact of his responses on the executive. Listening is simply to take in the information from the executive and deal with it and see how it lands on the executive.

Active listening is one of the communication techniques that is very useful for managers in day-to-day work while dealing with their subordinates. Active listening requires that the listener is to give feedback on what he hears from the speaker, by way of restating or paraphrasing what he has heard in his own words, to confirm what he has heard. The term active listening actually means the ability to pick up, define, and respond accurately to the feeling expressed by the other person.

In active listening, the manager (coach) tries to understand what his employee is feeling and what the employee's (executive client) message actually means. Then the manager puts his understanding of the message into his own words and repeats to the employee for verification. Hence active listening has two components:

1. Identification of feelings expressed
2. Feedback of content of message

Feelings emerge in the emotional tone that the speaker (employee/executive client) expresses, such as anger, joy, frustration, fear, surprise, disillusion, etc., whereas contents refer to ideas, reasons, assumptions, descriptions, etc., i.e., the substance of the speaker's message. When a manager is using active listening skillfully, the employee perceives that he is being understood. This perception frees the executive/employee to explore his own feelings and to express his own ideas.

Let us look an example of active listening:

> Executive Client (Employee): I just don't know how I am going to complete all the pending work on my desk before close of the month, especially since I am not sure how to deal with all these complex issues, pending for so long for one reason or the other.
>
> Coach (Manager): You are feeling frustrated and stuck with all the pending tasks as you do not know how to do and you are worried that you may not able to deal with them before close of the month.

In many conversations, the employee expresses troublesome feelings. In such occasions, just verbalizing these feelings clears the air and the employee feels at ease. In general, when a manager uses active listening, the executive/employee feels encouraged to think for oneself to diagnose the underlying causes and discover solutions by themselves.

Active listening is a powerful communication technique that prevents deterioration of self-esteem of the executive/employee and acts as a diffuser in emotional exchange. The active listening process can have threefold advantages:

1. It can increase the listener's understanding of the other person.
2. It can help clarify the thoughts and feelings of the speaker.
3. It can reassure the speaker that someone is willing to attend to their points of view and willing to help.

Here are some tips on what a manager (or coach) can do to listen to his employees (or executive client):

1. Remain silent when your employee is speaking. It is extremely difficult to receive information when there is noise or distraction. Active listening is attending to and tuning in to what the employee is talking.
2. Give the employee your undivided attention and acknowledge the message. Show your employee that you are listening. You may nod occasionally or encourage your employee to continue speaking with verbal cues, like "yes," "ok," etc. The manager needs to be centered in the present moment so that he can pay attention to what is being said.
3. To test your understanding of what you heard, restate the message in your own words. However, it is important to know exactly how and when to paraphrase. It is important to paraphrase major points in the conversation. Paraphrasing is a reflection of what has been said. The manager may do paraphrasing by saying, "What I am hearing is ..." More details on paraphrasing are given in this chapter.
4. Check your perceptions whether you could capture the emotional component in the conversation. Many a times, we miss the feelings expressed by the employee, since we

are too focused on the contents of the message. The coach may check the perceptions of feelings by saying: "It sounds as if you are really upset on what happened yesterday in the meeting."

5. Pause for a few seconds before replying to what the employee has just said. So often we jump to react to what we have just heard not ensuring whether the executive/employee is finished. There is an acronym that corporate coaches sometimes use to remind themselves to wait. It stands for "Why Am I Talking (WAIT)?" Sometimes, an extended pause may prompt the employee to think more about the issue compose their thoughts and share more details on the issue.

6. Don't judge your employee immediately. We may think that we know best what our employee should do, but the truth is it may not be true all the time. Our judgments and opinion may impair our listening, and hence we may pick up parts of conversation that are personally interesting and tune out parts that we deem boring or repetitive, which ultimately may become a very important piece of the conversation.

A corporate coach makes a conscious effort to hear not only the words what the executive is saying but, more importantly, try to understand the complete message being sent. The coach responds to the executive in a way that will encourage him or her to continue speaking, so that the coach can get the information they need in the coaching journey. The coach gives acknowledgment to the executive by simply a nod of the head or a simple "uh huh." While nodding or saying "uh huh," the coach communicates the message to the executive that he is interested and trying to understand the message well. The coach may not necessarily agree everything with the executive is saying, but simply indicating to the executive that he is being listened to. Using body language and other signs of acknowledgment, the coach normally tunes in to what the executive is saying and not to get distracted by whatever else may be going on around.

A coach listens for what the executive is saying, what they are not saying, how they are saying, what feelings or emotions are being expressed, what excites them, what are their stories, and what keeps them going or blocking them. A coach discovers in coaching conversation, through listening, how the executive is feeling, what the executive is really trying to say, which emotions are genuine, and what is really happening with the executive at that moment. A good coach is able to listen to the executive to a deeper level as to what is being felt by the executive.

Sometimes, the coach is required to listen to what's behind the words being said by the executive. Words describe our reality, what we interpret our world as being like, although it may not be immediately apparent. True listening can provide the insight to the coach when help is needed to the executive to shift perspectives that may be harming them. The central purpose of listening is to understand someone's point of view, how they think and feel, and how they move through the world. The coach also listens for what would fulfill their dreams and hopes, and for what may be getting on the way of reaching their dreams.

When the coach listens from the heart, not merely words the executive is saying, the coach also gets sensation in his own body. The coach then listens to their own body, takes notices of the sensation in their body to check what it is telling about the executive. It is important for the coaches to share these messages, feelings, or sensations with the executive to check what exactly the executive is telling and feeling.

To ensure that the coach understood what the executive is saying, the coach may ask interruptive questions like, "I need to understand what you are saying." "Tell me more…." or "Can you elaborate?" or "Is there anything else you want to say about this?" The coach may also say, "Let me see if I have got it right. You said that … Is that what you are saying?"

Whitworth et al. (2004) presented a model of three levels of listening. These three levels of listening give the coach an enormous range and, ultimately, a greater capacity for listening.

LEVEL 1: INTERNAL LISTENING

At level 1, the focus is on oneself and the own thoughts of the listener rather than the speaker. As the speaker is talking, the coach interprets what he hears in terms of what it means to him. The conversation is listened to and interpreted in terms of what it means to the listener. Here the focus is on listening selectively on the content of the messages, which are relevant to the listener.

Level 1 listening is all about ourselves and what's going around us. Executives are usually at level 1. It is their thoughts, their judgment, and their conclusions. Level 1 is normal everyday conversation, where it is natural for the listener to gather information to form opinions and make decisions. While listening at this level, the self-talk is very active.

There are many situations where level 1 listening is appropriate. You, as manager, are attending presentation by a third-party supplier or attending review meeting with other colleagues. All the attention of yours is on yourself. You are thinking about what information is being shared in the meeting, what are the issues relevant to you, how you will deal with data available with you, or how you are going to respond if some questions are raised or what question you will ask or may be what additional details need to be collected.

However, a coach will not be listening at this level; after all, a coaching session is not about the coach; it is about the executive and their needs. However, there are times when it may be appropriate, e.g., when the coach wants to decide a convenient time for the next coaching session. In this instance, the coach may need to take into account his own availability and make a judgment in order to agree on a mutually convenient time. The self-talk might be saying, do not fit the session in, if it is not possible for you to adjust it.

LEVEL 2: FOCUSED LISTENING

As a listener operating at level 2, the coach is focusing totally on the speaker, listening to their words, tone of voice, and body language and is not distracted by his/her own thoughts and feelings. Energy and information come from the executive and they are reflected back. The coach is like a mirror: what comes from the executive is returned back. Occasionally, we may see people engrossed in a conversation, when the listener is leaning forward, fully attentive. All the messages, verbal and nonverbal, being conveyed to the coach are being noticed. The executive will feel understood and the coach's own thoughts will not influence the coaching session.

By listening at level 2, if you are a manager, you can get a real understanding of where the employee is "coming from." You not only hear the words but also notice the tone, the pace, the feelings expressed. You hear their voice, their expressions, their emotions, their energy, their excitement, or disappointment. Active listening skill, discussed earlier in this chapter, will be most useful at level 2. You notice not only what they are saying but also how they are saying.

At this level, corporate coaches are unattached to self, their agenda, their thoughts, or their judgments. Corporate coach will be using this level of listening in the coaching sessions, with all the focus on the executive and the mind being concentrated on the words, tone, and body language of the executive. The coach's attention is what to say next, or what powerful question to pose to the executive, and when.

LEVEL 3: GLOBAL LISTENING

Listening at level 3 involves when the listener is focusing on the speaker and picking up more than what is being said. When coaching, the corporate coach will be listening to everything available using intuition, picking up emotion, and sensing signals from the executive's body language. It involves "listening at 360 degrees" to everything available, i.e., outside stimuli, feelings, emotions, and sensing signals. The coach trusts his senses, "goes with the flow," and responds that seems appropriate. The coach can gauge the energy of the executive and their emotions as well as picking up what they are not saying. The coach will understand what they are thinking and feeling, and trusting their own senses, he can be extremely responsive to the needs of the executive, knowing what question to ask next.

At level 3, intuition is very important. The coach will respond based on his/her intuitions. Then the coach will notice how his/her responses land on the executive. What is the impact of the responses on the executive? The key to listening at level 3 is to take information as it comes, use owns intuitions, play with it, and notice what emerges.

If you are a corporate trainer, you might have used level 3 listening. When you take training session, you are able to instantly read the impact you have created in a room by your delivery or presentation and adjust your behavior accordingly. Successful leaders master their listening skill at level 3 so that they can influence their executives/employees and make an impact.

Listening is one of the most important skills for corporate coaches. Listening is the entry point for any coaching process, through which all coaching passes. However, in some situations, some executives might talk continuously, repeating their stories again and again or try not to address the issues being discussed, or go on long discourse. Sometimes it seems irrelevant but can be a roundabout way of the executive to say what they need to say. A coach may decide to interrupt his executive or keep silent over a long period of time.

Finally, the objective of coaching is moving into action. As the coach listens, he makes choices on the directions and focus of coaching. However, only listening to the executive and giving them time and space of being heard are not enough, if there is no action after discussion, since it is not coaching at all.

Successful leaders know the importance of listening in managing their team. They listen more than they speak. They listen deeply and intently to the executive speaking to them. Their executives normally say, "My boss really took me seriously.... I felt as if I was the only person in the room in whom he is interested.... Those few minutes, I felt valued, appreciated and the center of attraction."

Reframing

Framing normally means a structure, a border, or a case for enclosing something. Take the example of a window frame or a photo frame, where the window or the photo is given support and protection by a frame. Reframing literarily means to frame it again.

All of us are only able to perceive or see a tiny part of the world around us. We develop our views, perspectives, beliefs, and assumptions based on limited experience and knowledge of the world. This perception then leads us to subscribe different meanings to different situations, as we encounter. Our feelings and behaviors then accordingly determine how to deal with a situation. If we change the way we view a situation, then we can view different situations from different viewpoints or perspectives.

In the coaching context, a frame is the current or present perspective the executive may have. Here we need to see framing, as how the executive provides structure and support to his/her current thoughts, beliefs, perceptions, perspectives, and actions. Reframing, therefore, helps the executive to see that there could be different perspectives, thoughts, or beliefs, which may be more appropriate, empowering, or relevant in the given situation. Reframing gives the executives the leverage to explore different options they might have.

The executives are entitled to new perspectives or point of view, review their own behavior, action, or assumptions. They can check their own beliefs, resources, or assets they have or do not have and then identify the more empowering ones, which make the executive move forward. These new perspectives, thoughts, beliefs, perceptions, or realizations are required to be framed. This needs adequate support and protection in the way they deal with different situations.

One of the important roles of a coach is to help the executive get clarity on their current perspectives. The coach helps them see whether the current perspective is working for them or not. If the current perspective is not working for the executive, then the coach enthuses the executive to look at the situation from a different perspective or viewpoint and identify which perspective is more empowering than the perspective that he/she currently holds.

When the executives identify a new perspective, then the coach helps the executives to develop a framework or a structure to direct their behaviors and actions in alignment with the new perspective. When we identify a new perspective to deal with a situation, then our behaviors, actions, and feelings originate from the reframed perspective.

It is important to note that while the coach is reframing, the situation does not change, but the perspective or way of looking at the situation only changes. It is also not necessary that in all situations the mindset or paradigm will change in reframing, but it may facilitate the process. As long as the executive is reframing or examining his or her own perspectives, the executive feels empowered while exploring.

Some of the reframing questions could be:

1. Can you understand this from another person's perspective?
2. Have you tried to see this situation from another or a completely opposite point of view?
3. What is the worst thing that could happen in this situation?
4. What will it take to reach this particular objective/idea?
5. If you were up for a breakthrough, what would you do?
6. What is missing here, that if included would make this situation look like?
7. What could you do that will make you "go where no one has gone before"?
8. How could this be fun?
9. What are the most enjoyable aspects about this?
10. What perspective could you take now that could empower you to solve it?
11. Let's look at this in a different light to understand this situation better.
12. In what way can the current situation be made perfect?
13. What can you do better?
14. If you had a choice, what would you do?
15. What will you do if it does not work?

Powerful Questions

A question can be a coach's most valuable tool in assisting executives to think clearly and solve problems. Questions help in the problem-solving process. Powerful questions "dig in" deeper and open our thoughts to explore ideas even further. Coaches, who encourage the executives to elaborate on and explain their thinking through the use of probing questions, promote learning because such questions push executives to think more deeply about what they are dealing with in their life.

Thinking critically involves a process of reason and discernment through a set of questions. By responding to questions, we discern a set of answers. When the trail leads to the answer, we can uncover more truths by searching each answer to see if it presents a new set of questions. This question-and-answer methodology for discerning truth is nothing new. It is commonly referred to as the "Socrates Method" and derives its name from the ancient Greek philosopher, Socrates. He would constantly pose questions to his listeners to trigger thinking in the right direction. Questioning continued until the listeners provided the most logical answer to a particular problem and discovery followed.

Probing questions, such as, "Why?" "Can you elaborate?" "What evidence can you present to support your answer?," etc., encourage the executives to "unpack" their thinking and show how they have reached particular conclusions. This process can be viewed as peeling an onion with each question unwrapping a new layer. Coaches use probing questions to encourage their executives to consider and weigh diverse evidences. It also allows the executive to examine the validity of their own deductive and inductive ways of thinking.

Probing questions are used for the executives to extend their knowledge beyond factual recall, to apply what is known, what is unknown, and to elaborate on what is known. By "peeling the onion" and getting to the heart of a matter, executives are more likely to find their own "truths," which help them develop their goals that are aligned with these truths and act on these goals.

If a corporate coach wants his executive to reflect further on a problem or view it from a different angle, some of the most powerful questions are:

1. "How can I best coach you in this situation?"
2. "What would be the best question to ask you right now to help you think clearly about this situation?"
3. "What is the lesson here?"
4. "What do you need to do now?"

If you think someone is holding back through fear or insecurity, some of the best questions to ask are:

1. "What are you resisting?"
2. "Have you been here before?"
3. "Are you holding on to something you need to let go off perhaps?"
4. "What are you not telling me?"

OPEN- AND CLOSE-ENDED QUESTIONS

A close-ended question is one in which there are a limited number of acceptable answers, usually, "yes" or "no." Examples of close-ended questions are:

1. "Did you have a good week?"
2. "Did you do your fieldwork?"

An open-ended question is one in which there are many acceptable answers, thus providing an opportunity for the executive to elaborate. Examples of open-ended questions are:

1. "Tell me about your week?"
2. "What was your experience with the fieldwork?"

For coaching conversation to continue and to ensure that the coaching is executive-centered, the coaches ask generally open-ended questions. It is also important that after asking a question to the executive, the coach needs to have patience till the executive responds. If the coach does not allow enough time between asking a question and expecting an answer, then the coach is not effectively questioning. Unless the coach leaves sufficient wait time when an executive ceases speaking, then the coach is not listening effectively and the quality of the information the coach gets back will reflect that. Similarly, the coach may be met with silence from the executives when the coach asks a question—this could be because the executives have not understood the question or they are thinking through the question the coach has asked. Some coaches get tempted to ask another question or rephrase the first question, which is not desirable in coaching conversation. After asking thought-provoking question to the executives, silence gives the executives the space to think through their responses they would give. In a normal conversation, a period of silence is usually uncomfortable. In a coaching conversation, silence is natural—there is no pressure on the coach, since he is there to listen to his executive.

Silence could be a golden moment in coaching session. An effective coach creates golden moments by recognizing when silence is better than asking further questions. An ineffective coach rushes with follow-up questions, not giving enough pause or time to think for the executive for reflection. During the time to think, i.e., pause or silence between two questions, the executive gets the opportunity to reflect deeply what are being discussed, what he just said or not said, what to do next, etc.

Finally, questioning is really just an extension of listening. Questioning only occurs in response to what the executive is saying. Questions are tools that need to be used strategically and purposefully by the coach to support the executive on their learning journey. However, each executive's journey will be unique. The coach's overall goal is to move the dialog in a direction that assists the executive to meet his or her goals. Annexure 8.1 gives a list of powerful questions, which a coach can use in coaching conversation.

Effective Feedback

Each one of us wants real feedback from those who are important in our life. It is true in coaching too. The executives want their coaches to point out things they are overlooking or missing. The coach sees what the executives are not able to see. Giving constructive feedback to the executive can be an extremely valuable component in coaching, if it is done properly. Effective feedback creates a kind of awareness that makes a difference in how the executive sees things. Feedback in coaching helps the executives increase their awareness on what they are doing, how they are doing, and the impact of their behavior on others. 360-degree feedback is one such tool that generally captures these aspects of the executive. When the coach gives feedback effectively, it fuels motivation to the executive to improve performance.

Feedback is neither positive nor negative. Feedback is always neutral and objective. Feedback in coaching is the statement from the coach on how a coach observes, sees, or notices things as it happens. It is just mirroring it back to the executive the way the coach notices it. This means that the feedback is just information, free of value judgments. While giving feedback to the executives, the coaches do not offer their opinions, judgment, or beliefs but just give the executives an insight they may need. When giving feedback, the greatest challenge one can have is to really make a contribution that benefits the executive. It involves giving up judgments, opinions, and even beliefs about something or someone.

The ultimate purpose of feedback in coaching is to empower the executive for further actions and growth. If an executive shares a situation, the coach can offer to provide feedback by saying: "Would you like a different perspective?" or "Can I share with you what I am getting from that?" Hence, feedback is simply about sharing an observation without judgment or opinion. An opinion sounds more like this: "Well let me tell you what I think about that!"

The following points are important in giving feedback during coaching:

1. The coach always asks permission before giving feedback to the executive by asking, "May I offer you some feedback," "Would you like me to give some feedback," etc. When the executive grants permission to the coach for giving feedback, the executive will be more receptive to listen what the coach is saying. It is also important for the executive to know that the feedback is only from the coach's perspectives.

2. The coach should be honest, truthful, and humble while giving feedback to the executive. The coach shares truthfully his/her own experiences as an example from which to learn from.

3. The coaches are sensitive to the feelings and emotions of the executive. The coach imagines how he would have felt if he were at the receiving end.

4. Effective feedback involves a proper structure, proper choice of words, the manner, tone, and pace of delivery. Giving feedback, which will make the biggest difference to the executive, requires a lot of practice.

5. The timing of the feedback in the coaching is also important. The coach waits for appropriate moments for giving feedback to the executive, when the executive is ready for feedback. An effective coach will give very few feedbacks during the coaching process, but each feedback is quality feedback, well thought-of and specific so that the executive gets benefitted from the coach's feedback.

6. Coaches own the power of their words. They are quite responsible for what and how they provide feedback. For instance, to declare how the coach feels about something, the coach may say, "When you said that, I felt sad because ..."

7. Coaches are aware of their opinions and judgments and then let them go. The viewpoint of the coach will not always make the biggest difference to the executives because their point of view may be different from that of the coachee's.

8. It is possible that the executive may sometimes ignore the feedback given by their coach. It does not mean that the coach will not give feedback or their feedback is not making

any impact. The coach actually plants seeds in the executive's mind that takes time to sprout. Sometimes, the coach needs to share what he notices, so the executive can think about it and take action.

However, giving performance feedback to executives/employees by their manager is quite different from what corporate coach gives feedback to their executives. Performance feedback is the ongoing communication process between executive/employee and manager where information is exchanged concerning the performance expected and the performance exhibited. Feedback is an essential part of improving performance, regardless of current performance levels of their employees. Only through performance feedback, the employees become aware whether they are on track and doing the right thing. Performance feedback is not only provided to the employees when the performance is off the track but also to give recognition to the employees on their accomplishment. However giving effective performance feedback is an important skill and not something that is "natural" to every manager. Giving employees honest feedback on their performance can be one of the toughest jobs a manager can do. Many managers often shy away from delivering honest feedback to their executives/employees because it is uncomfortable and can seem overwhelming to deal with. Yet without good feedback the employees cannot grow and learn. Some managers use the performance feedback as an opportunity only to highlight negative performance or to be used as a platform to criticize their employees or just to clear the air. It is not desirable. It creates a de-motivating environment for the employees. The performance feedback is given to employees only for improving the performance of the employees. If it is not so, then managers should avoid giving performance feedback.

The following tips are helpful for managers while giving performance feedback to their employees:

Create the right setting: All performance feedback sessions should be conducted in a private, one-on-one setting, behind a closed door, without interruptions. Never give feedback to an executive/employee in a setting where other executives/employees may overhear the conversation. Feedback on the employee's performance should be a private discussion between the manager and the executive/employee to whom it concerns. This is a simple rule, but many managers underestimate the value of privacy in dealing with their executives/employees and risk of damaging the trust of the employee–manager relationship. If a manager does not give his employee complete and undivided attention, a clear signal is conveyed to the employee that this conversation is not all that important.

Address performance problems honestly and directly: The manager needs to address performance problems honestly and directly. The performance feedback should be as specific as possible. The manager must describe the situation with facts and figures, which the executive/employee is aware of. If a manager has not observed a performance problem directly, it should not be addressed in performance feedback. While presenting the performance problem to the employee, the manager should focus on facts, not on the person. Feedback is most effective when manager writes down the feedback he is going to give to the executive/employee, before meeting the executive/employee.

Ask the employee: The manager should get the employee's point of view of the situation and how it can be improved. When employees are given a chance to comment on their own behavior and productivity, the employees are likely to be tougher on themselves and they will also work harder to improve in the areas they commit personally. The manager also needs to be open to listen to the views of the employee and may need to change his own perception or opinion, if need be.

Communicate expectations clearly: Performance expectations need to be delivered in a concise, clear manner, without questionable interpretations, especially when there is a problem. Numbers, dates, productivity units, metrics, and standards are helpful to include when communicating specific performance expectations to an executive/employee. The more specific the manager is, the less misinterpretation by the employee is likely to occur.

Include the positives: Employees need encouragement and to be told when they are doing well. Many managers are so concerned about correcting their executives'/employees' mistakes that they tend to overlook their positive achievements altogether. It is important to recognize employees for their accomplishments to keep them motivated. Another common mistake is to overwhelm employees with a long laundry list of areas to improve. A better approach is to identify two or three of the most critical areas to improve, and allow the employee to focus on improving these.

Develop an action plan to resolve the situation: The managers and the employees should finally decide what actions the employees are going to take, what help is required from the managers, and how the follow-up will be done.

Mirroring

The function of a mirror is reflection. All of us look into a mirror to see what we are projecting ourselves to others and how they are seeing us. Therefore mirroring, in simple terms, is reflecting what the executive is doing or saying while communicating with the coach. When the coach acts as a mirror, he plays a role of reflecting back to the executive what his realities are. Normally, the coach displays the same expression, same words, same tone of voice, etc., as an executive exhibits while communicating with the coach. It could be the facial expression, the physical positions, the body postures, mannerism, or verbal communication style.

Examples:

1. The executive is tense and speaking slowly, taking time between sentences, breathing heavily while conversing with the coach. The coach mirrors back the same, speaks slowly, and gives pauses during the conversation.

2. The executive uses the word "you see" quite frequently. The
    coach mirrors back the same by using word "I see" frequently
    instead of "I hear" or "I understand."

The purpose of mirroring is to build rapport with an executive.
When a coach subtly mirrors the executive, the executive tends
to become friendlier and open toward the coach. In a sense, the
executives view the coach as their own mirror. During coaching,
the coach mirrors their executive to give the message to the executive that he is hearing him. This helps the coach present an objective
reality of the situation.

The mirroring technique can also be used effectively by a coach
when the coach would like to reflect back the executive's words,
stories, emotions, etc. so that they can become aware or bring attention to what they are saying and thinking so that they have choices
to revalidate their perspectives.

Sometimes, the executive makes some judgmental statement
about how they view themselves or how they judge themselves
without giving sufficient thoughts or introspection. Then, the
coach mirrors back exactly all the words what he heard from the
executive, without adding or changing any word, with a tone of
questioning. When the executive hears it back from the coach, then
they explore whether that is what they really meant. This leads to
creating awareness within the executive of something they want
to change, reflect, or introspect. The mirroring by the coach also
provides an opportunity for the executives to articulate their own
perspectives or mindset.

Sometimes, mirroring by the coach triggers an immediate
response from the executive. The executive may explain what he
actually meant through examples of situations. This process of mirroring provides a safe environment to the executive, wherein they
revalidate their own judgments or perspective or what they have
just said. They also revalidate its relevance whether for a specific to
a context or a situation or in general.

To sum up, in the mirroring process, the executive gets an opportunity to explore his perspective. It is important to mention here that mirroring is not mimicking, but is a skill that needs to be acquired.

Paraphrasing

Paraphrasing means to state the understanding coaches acquire from executives in their own words. Hence, paraphrasing involves editing and summarizing the words being said by the executive to the coach. To begin paraphrasing, the coach might start by saying "what I hear you saying is ...," or "what I understood is ..." or "let me see if I have understood you properly ..." or "from what you said, I gather that ...," etc.

The benefit of paraphrasing is to communicate to the executive that his message is getting across to the coach. The executives also appreciate the fact that they are being understood by their coach. It also prevents any misunderstanding between the coach and the executive. There is a sense of comfort and easiness in all the subsequent conversations between the coach and the executive.

Paraphrasing is an important part in active listening process of coaching. Active listening has mainly two components: what is being said or not said, i.e., content of the communication and identification of the feelings, as expressed by the executive while communicating.

In active listening, the coach tries to understand what the executive is feeling internally or what the executive's message really meant. The coach's active listening response is then putting his own understanding of the message into his own words and communicating back to the executive for verification, which is actually paraphrasing. An active listening response provides a sense of comfort to the executive that he is being fully understood including his feelings and emotions involved in this situation.

Mirroring by coach is done to help executives understand or examine their own perspectives and, if necessary, to reframe their perspective so that they can move in the direction they want to be.

In contrast, paraphrasing by coach does not create an opportunity for the executives to reframe their perspective, but are able to create an enabling climate for coaching.

Chapter Summary

While communicating with an executive, coaches use different communication techniques like active listening, giving feedback, power listening, and powerful questioning. These tools are used to build rapport, to create mutual understanding, to understand the perspectives and issues an executive is facing, and also to create an environment conducive for coaching.

Listening is an important tool for managers. When managers listen to their executives/employees skillfully, they convey a message to them that they care about them. Listening is not hearing. Listening happens through six distinct processes: hearing, attending, understanding, remembering, evaluating, and responding. While listening to their executive, the coaches not only hear the words the executive is speaking, but also pay attention to the tone, the body posture, expressions, energy, and the feelings expressed. Active listening is an important skill for managers in dealing with their subordinates. In active listening, managers try to understand the content of the message what their executives/employees are trying to communicate and the feelings being expressed by the executives/employees. Then they restate what they have heard in their own words to confirm their understanding. This helps the manager send a message to his executives/employees he is trying to understand their points of views or issues, which act as diffuser in emotional exchange between the manager and the subordinates as well as prevent deterioration of self-esteem of the executives/employees. In coaching, the listening happens at three levels: Internal listening, focused listening and global listening. At the level of internal listening, the coach interprets what he hears in terms of what means to him, i.e., focus is not on the executive. At the level of focused listening, the coach is focusing totally on the speaker, listening to the words, tone of voice, and body language of the executive. Here, the coach works like a mirror, what comes from the executive is reflected back to the executive. During global listening, the coach listens at 360 degree (i.e., listening more than what is being said). The coach also picks up emotions and sensing signals from the body of the coachee. Deep coaching conversation happens at level 2 and level 3 of listening.

Reframing in coaching refers to giving new or different perspective to executives by their coach. Reframing helps the executive explore that there could be different perspectives, thoughts, or points of view for a given situation, which may be more appropriate or empowering for them. During coaching, the coaches encourage their executives whether their own perspective is working for them or not. If not, the coach enthuses the executives to examine the situation from a different perspective or viewpoint, so that they can leverage different options they might have.

Powerful questions help the coach assist their executive to think clearly and solve their problems by their own answer. Coach asks probing but powerful questions during coaching to ensure that the executives think more deeply on the issues they are facing. The Socratic method of questioning is the most powerful tool in coaching, in which he would constantly pose questions to his disciple after each answer until they provide the most logical answer to a particular problem.

Feedback in coaching means mirroring it back to executives what the coach observes, sees, or notices things as they happen, without any opinion or judgment from the coach. Coaching executives want their coach to give them feedback so that they are able to see what they are missing or overlooking. The objective of giving effective feedback in coaching is to empower executives for their further action and growth. In organizations, managers are expected to give performance feedback to their subordinates. However, giving performance feedback is a skill that needs to be learnt and mastered.

Mirroring and paraphrasing are other important communication tools for coaching. Mirroring is reflecting back to the executives what the coach observes so that they can examine the current reality of their situation. In paraphrasing, coaches state in their own words what they acquire from the executive in the conversation to create a proper understanding of the executive's situation as well as an enabling environment for coaching.

Annexure 8.1: 150+ Powerful Questions

1. What are the possibilities?
2. If you had your choice, what would you do?
3. What are the possible solutions?
4. What if you do and what if you do not?
5. What do you make of it all?
6. What do you think? (is the best?)
7. How does it look to you?
8. How do you feel about it?
9. What led up to _____?
10. What have you tried so far?
11. What do you make of it all?
12. What do you mean?
13. What does it look/sound/feel like?
14. What seems to confuse you?
15. What was it like?
16. What happened?
17. Then what?
18. In what way?
19. How does this fit with your plans/ways of life/values?
20. What do you think?
21. For instance?
22. Like what?
23. Such as?
24. What else?
25. What other ideas do you have about it?
26. What if it does not work out the way you wish?
27. What if that does not work?
28. And if that fails, what will you do?
29. How do you want it to be?
30. If you could do it over again, what would you do differently?
31. If it were you, what would you have done?
32. How else could a person handle this?
33. If you could do anything you wanted, what would you do?
34. What seems to be the trouble?

35. What seems to be the main obstacle?
36. What is stopping you?
37. What concerns you most about _____?
38. What will you have to do to get the job done?
39. What support do you need to accomplish _____?
40. What will you do?
41. By when will you do it?
42. What information do you need before you decide?
43. What do you know about it now?
44. How do you suppose you can find out more about it?
45. What kind of picture do you have right now?
46. How do you explain this to yourself?
47. What was the lesson/learning?
48. How can you lock it (the learning) in?
49. How would you pull all this together?
50. What was your part in this?
51. How do you fit into the picture?
52. What were you responsible for?
53. If you had free choice in the matter, what would you do?
54. If the same thing came up again, what would you do?
55. If we could wipe the slate clean, what would you do?
56. If you had it to do over again, what would you do?
57. What would you like to focus on today?
58. What would you like coaching on today?
59. What would you like to explore today?
60. What do you want?
61. What is your desired outcome?
62. If you got it, what would you have?
63. How will you know you have accomplished it?
64. When you are 95 years old, what will you want to say about your life?
65. What would you like to be doing five years from now?
66. What is your life purpose?
67. In the bigger scheme of things, how important is this?
68. What do you plan to do about it?
69. What is your game plan?

70. What kind of plan do you need to create?
71. How do you suppose you could improve the situation?
72. How do you suppose it will all work out?
73. What will that get you?
74 Where will this lead?
75. What are the chances of success?
76. If you do this, how will it affect _____?
77. What impact will that have on balance/values?
78. How does this affect the whole picture?
79. What else do you need to take into consideration?
80. What action will you take? And after that?
81. What will you do? When?
82. Where do you go from here? When will you do that?
83. What are your next steps? By when?
84. How is this working? How is this going?
85. How would you describe this?
86. What do you think this all amounts to?
87. How would you summarize the work/effort so far?
88. How could this be fun?
89. What is most enjoyable about this?
90. What have you accomplished in your life?
91. What to be coached on? How can I help? How can I support you?
92. What will make a big difference in your life?
93. What is the number one thing you would like most to have in your life?
94. What you wanted to have, not got it?
95. What motivates you?
96. What have you done about this so far?
97. What is missing in the situation?
98. What is holding you back?
99. What is really going on *(Intuition)*?
100. What you did for which you are proud of?
101. How you had dealt with similar situations before?
102. What talent you have so that you can make that happen?
103. What is preventing you?

104. What is the number one thing you got of this session?
105. Why that is important to you?
106. How this situation could be perfect?
107. What can you change?
108. How other people may look at this situation differently?
109. What meaning/different meaning you can attach to it?
110. What you want to walk out today evening?
111. Can you understand this from another person's perspective?
112. Have you tried to see this situation from another or a completely opposite point of view?
113. What is the worst thing that could happen in this situation?
114. What will it take to reach this particular objective/idea?
115. If you were up for a breakthrough, what would you do?
116. What is missing here, which if included would make this situation look like?
117. What could you do that will make you "go where no one has gone before?"
118. How could this be fun?
119. What are the most enjoyable aspects about this?
120. What perspective could you take now that could empower you to solve it?
121. Let's look at this in a different light to understand this situation better?
122. In what way can the current situation be made perfect?
123. What can you do better?
124. If you had a choice, what would you do?
125. What will you do if it does not work?
126. What structure you can put in place that you are in motion?
127. What are some personal boundaries you would like to have?
128. What steps will you take to ensure that your new perspectives are aligned with your values?
129. What would help you to find the first step?
130. How can you get the information/knowledge you need?
131. What could you do now if you knew you could not fall?
132. Is it the right time to make a commitment to achieve these goals?

133. What would you have to do to get the job done?
134. How would you know that you have accomplished it?
135. What is your game plan?
136. What do you consider to be your greatest strengths?
137. What do you consider to be your greatest weaknesses?
138. What kinds of activities/goals/situations make you feel most motivated/confident and/or happy?
139. What have I learned about myself from others?
140. What you expect from the coach to do for you?
141. What are the challenges you are facing now or what you think you are stuck in?
142. What are the issues you would like to discuss in the next two or three sessions?
143. Anything else you would like your coach should know about you?
144. If you were to fully live your life, what is the first change you would start to make?
145. What could we work on now that would make the biggest difference to your life?
146. What are you tolerating/putting up with?
147. What do you want more of in your life?
148. What you want less of in your life?
149. What are the three things you are doing regularly that don't serve or support you?
150. What do you love?
151. What do you hate?
152. What's the one thing you would love to do before?
153. What is the aim of discussion?
154. What does success look like?
155. Is that possible, challenging, attainable?

Reference

Whitworth, L., Kimsey-House, H., & Sandahl, P. (2004). *Co-active coaching; new skills for coaching people towards success in work and life*. Palo Alto, California: Davis-Black Publishing.

CHAPTER 9

Psychometrics and Psychological Inventories in Corporate Coaching

Psychometrics is the science of measuring behavior and ability adhering to the four psychometric principles, i.e., reliability, validity, standardization, and freedom from bias. Wikipedia defines psychometrics as

> the field of study concerned with the theory and technique of psychological measurement, which includes the measurement of knowledge, abilities, attitudes, personality traits, and educational measurement. The field is primarily concerned with the construction and validation of measurement instruments such as questionnaires, tests and personality assessments.

There is widespread use of psychometric tools in recruitment and selection, assessment center, and leadership development. Corporate coaches are increasingly using psychometric instruments in coaching with the permission of the executives. The reasons for using psychometrics tools in coaching are varied but most of the coaches use psychometric instruments to enable themselves to adjust their coaching style based on their own strengths, styles, or preferences vis-à-vis those of the executive. Psychometric instruments are also used to gather additional data and perspectives of the executive, so that coaches can structure their coaching process accordingly. On the other hand, the psychometric data help executives to get awareness on who they are, what gift they have, what are their styles or preferences, and what are their developmental needs. Good psychological instruments, if used appropriately by the coaches, can be useful tools to support the corporate coaching executives in building awareness through self-exploration and understanding.

This chapter gives an overview of some, not all, of the common psychometric instruments being used in coaching. All the psychometric instruments covered in this chapter have strong evidence of psychometric properties including high reliability and validity. New coaches are advised to see the eligibility criteria of test administration and interpretation from the test publisher, since there are strict ethical guidelines for administration and interpretation. Users of these inventories are advised to get themselves trained and certified for administration and interpretation as well get themselves informed and knowledgeable about the limitations and capabilities of each test they might like to use.

Myers-Briggs Type Indicator

The Myers-Briggs Type Indicator (MBTI) is a self-report questionnaire designed to identify variable differences between normal and healthy people. It is based on psychological type theory developed by the Swiss psychiatrist Carl G. Jung. Jung observed that the differences in behavior result from people's inborn tendencies to use their minds in different ways. As people act on these tendencies, they develop specific patterns of behavior. The essence of the theory is that much seemingly random variation in behavior is actually quite orderly and consistent, due to basic differences in the way individuals prefer to use their perception and judgment. Perception involves all the ways of becoming aware of things, people, happenings, or ideas. Judgment involves all the ways of coming to conclusion about what has been perceived. If people differ systematically in what they perceive and in how they reach conclusions, then it is only reasonable for them to differ correspondingly in their interests, reactions, values, motivations, and skills (Myers et al., 1998). Jung believed that people are innately different in what they prefer, and identified eight mental processes, called type preferences. Katharine Briggs and Isabel Myers' interpretation of the Jung idea of type preferences led to the development of the Myers-Briggs Type Indicators personality inventory.

The dynamic character specified by type theory involves the interaction of a person's four basic preferences (Myers et al., 1998). The MBTI theory focuses on the preferences on four dichotomies, each consisting of two opposite poles. It indicates that the differences in people result from the following:

1. When people prefer to focus their attention and get energy (extroversion, E, or introversion, I)
2. The way they prefer to take information (sensing, S, or intuition, N)
3. The way they prefer to make decisions (thinking, T or feeling, F)
4. How they orient themselves to the external world (judging, J, or perceiving, P)

Myers et al. (1998) note that a preference for one alternative of each dichotomy does not mean that the opposite, less-preferred alternative is never used. Both the theory and practical observations describe individuals as using each of the eight preference categories at least some of the time. The combination of four dichotomies yield 16 possible combinations, called Type, as given in Figure 9.1.

ISTJ	ISFJ	INFJ	INTJ
ISTP	ISFP	INFP	INTP
ESTP	ESFP	ENFP	ENTP
ESTJ	ESFJ	ENFJ	ENTJ

Source: Myers et al. (1998).

Figure 9.1 Sixteen Personality Types of MBTI

It is also important to understand that the type theories postulate that each type stands for a complex set of dynamic relationships among the functions (S, N, T, and F), the attitude (E and I), and the orientation to the outer world (J and P). Based on the Jungian basis of type dynamics, Myers and Briggs assumed the following:

1. For each type, one function (from S, N, T, and F) will be dominant. People of each type will mainly use their dominant function in their favorite attitude (E and I), i.e., extraverts use the dominant function in the outer world of extraversion.
2. In addition to the dominant function, the auxiliary function is developed to provide balance. For extraverts, the dominant function will be extraverted and the auxiliary function will typically be used in the inner world of introversion.
3. Extraverts show their best function, i.e., dominant function to the outside world, whereas introverts show their second-best function to the outer world.
4. The function opposed to dominant function is typically the least-developed or inferior function. The inferior function tends to be used in the less-preferred attitude (extraversion or introversion).
5. The function contrary to auxiliary function is called tertiary function and is used in the less-preferred attitude.

For example, ESTJ type will have Thinking (T) as dominant extroverted function and Sensing (S) will be auxiliary, introverted function. Hence, Feeling (F) is an inferior, introverted function (since it is opposite of Thinking, T). Intuition (N) is the tertiary function. Therefore, ESTJs take an objective approach to problem solving and are tough when the situation requires toughness. They use their Thinking primarily externally to organize their lives and work. They focus on the present what is real and actual. They apply and adapt relevant past experience to deal with problems, and they prefer jobs where results are immediate, visible, and tangible. They are likely to be:

1. Logical, analytical, and objectively critical
2. Decisive, clear, and assertive
3. Practical, realistic, and matter-of-fact

It is natural for ESTJs to give less attention to their non-preferred Feeling and Intuitive parts. They may:

1. Remain logical even when emotions and impacts on people need prime consideration
2. Not be able to see the wider ramifications of a seemingly simple, direct action
3. Fail to respond to others' needs for emotional intimacy and processing of feelings of others

Understanding type dynamics is important in MBTI. Since it is not possible to discuss the type dynamics for all types of MBTI, the coaches are recommended to refer the MBTI Manual, published by CPP Inc., for further understanding. Executives having the following combinations in their type may show the following characteristics at their workplace:

TJ: They are analytical and decisive leaders. They make decisions based on principle and systems, overall impacts, and rational assessment of outcomes and can be tough-minded in implementing decisions.

TP: They lead by examples. They value and display technical expertise and create orderly frameworks for working. They are objective, skeptical, and curious. They will change course as new information comes in.

FP: They are warm, flexible, and encouraging leaders. They support individual work styles and like to involve others in decision. They prefer collegial relationships, shared rewards, and consensus in decisions. They could be good internal coaches.

FJ: They are warm, decisive leaders. They make decisions based on their personal values and empathy with others. They strive for harmony, consensus, and a supportive environment.

Since each type has its own strengths and areas of developments, the coach assesses the executives from 16 personality type perspectives on what behavior is normal, comfortable, and valued and what is difficult, uncomfortable, and trivial for the executive. The coach gives the executives a sense of worth and dignity based on the gift they have, which they need to exploit further to achieve growth and excellence.

In coaching, the executive may focus on developing on tertiary and inferior functions. The experienced coach, having a complete understanding of MBTI, will instead encourage the executive to use dominant and auxiliary functions to strengthen the less-secure and more-inexperienced tertiary and inferior functions. The coach can help their executive identify their less-preferred functions and their level of discomfort with these functions and then make conscious use of tertiary and inferior functions through practice.

Fundamental Interpersonal Relations Orientation-Behavior (FIRO-B)

FIRO-B has been widely used in the fields of human relation since it was introduced in 1958 by Dr Will Schutz. Dr Will Schutz was called by US Navy during the Korean War and was given the task of creating a method for constructing effective teams. In the course of performing experiments to predict team compatibility, he devised the FIRO theory and the FIRO-B instrument. FIRO-B was designed to predict the level of interaction between two people.

The theory postulates that "people need people." People, being social beings, have interpersonal needs that may be satisfied through the attainment of a satisfactory relation with other people. The FIRO theory focuses on three major levels—behavior, feelings, and self-concept. FIRO-B is one such instrument on behavior. FIRO-B, a 54-item questionnaire, measures the behavioral aspects of the three dimensions of interpersonal relations; these are inclusion, control, and affection, which explain most of the human interactions. The FIRO-B theory assumes that the above three dimensions are fundamental in understanding and predicting interpersonal behavior. The scores on affection reflect the degree to which a person becomes emotionally connected with others. Inclusion assesses the degree to which a person associates himself/ herself with others. Control measures the extent to which a person assumes responsibility, makes decisions, or dominates people. Schutz (1958) defines three interpersonal needs as follows:

Inclusion: Inclusion is defined behaviorally as the need to establish and maintain a satisfactory relation with people with respect to interaction and association. High expressed inclusion scores reflect people would like to get associated, interact, mingle, belong, involve, look for companion, would like to join group or parties, outgoing, like to start conversation with strangers, and look for recognition. Low scores reflect that these people prefer exclusion, prefer to be alone, generally withdrawn or reserved, and they generally do not start conversation with others.

Control: Control is defined behaviorally as the need to establish and maintain a satisfactory relation with respect to control and power. High expressed control score reflects that they are comfortable when they are in charge. High expressed scores also mean they would like to have authority, dominance, rule, or bossing over others. Low score reflects that they prefer not to have control over others, they would prefer to be follower, or may not like to have responsibilities. It also reflects sometimes in rebellion or resistance or submissive attitudes.

Affection: Affection is defined as the need to establish and maintain a warm or emotional connection with others. They prefer to be close with others, develop personal relationship with others, be affectionate with others, give a feeling of intimacy, etc. Low expressed scores reflect that they prefer to remain cool, distance themselves, not get emotionally involved, etc. They will prefer to keep the relationship impersonal, avoid being open with people, and prefer to have acquaintances rather than a few close friends.

Table 9.1   FIRO-B Scales (0–9)

	Inclusion	Control	Affection
Expressed behavior	I initiate interaction with people	I control people	I act close and personal with people
Wanted behavior	I want to be included	I want people to control me	I want people to get close and personal with me

FIRO-B measures each dimension in two scales: expressed and wanted. The expressed score represents the manifested behavior, i.e., the observed behavior. The expressed behavior points to the level of behavior people are most comfortable in demonstrating toward others to bring people together, to get their way, and to be close to others. The wanted score represents what the person wants from other people. The Wanted aspect of each dimension points to the behavior people want or prefer others to do in their attempts to get together with them. Therefore, FIRO-B provides feedback on six aspects of interpersonal behavior, as given in Table 9.1.

The scores in each dimension range from 0 to 9. For the purpose of interpretation, scores of 0–3 are considered as low, 4–6 as moderate, and 7–9 as high. It is not possible to discuss how to interpret FIRO-B scores in details in this chapter. However, one case example is presented in this chapter so that the coaches can get an idea of how FIRO-B instrument can be used in corporate coaching for predicting interpersonal behavior of the executives.

Case Example: Executive R is working as head of marketing in an MNC organization. He is known as a strong team manager, and an ambitious and committed executive. His FIRO-B scores are as follows (Table 9.2):

Table 9.2   FIRO-B Scores

	Inclusion	Control	Affection
Expressed	5	1	6
Wanted	6	3	8

Contd.

Contd.

The overall interpersonal need scores are calculated by totaling all the numbers. It is 29 out of maximum possible 54. It can be concluded that this executive has moderate interpersonal needs. The overall strength of interpersonal need shows how much he believes that interaction with others can help him attain his goals and personal satisfaction.

His total scores on expressed behavior and wanted behaviors (rows and columns total) are 12 and 17, respectively. The total expressed behaviors score represents how much initiative he takes in approaching others to fulfill his three interpersonal needs, i.e., inclusion, control, and affection. Total wanted behavior score reflects how much he depends on others to get what he needs. Both these scores are in medium range; hence, his behaviors are moderate. However his wanted behavior score is higher than the expressed behavior, which indicates that he prefers to wait and see what others will do before initiating his actions. He may be hesitant being proactive, whereas he may be expecting that others should act toward him or waiting for others to act toward him.

Now if we calculate the total of each column, it emerges that the highest score is in the area of affection followed by inclusion and then control. It reflects that he would be more comfortable in building relationship and trust with others in a new situation before taking any action.

Now let us analyze his scores separately in three areas of interpersonal needs. His expressed score in inclusion is 5, whereas in wanted inclusion is 6. This score suggests that he is socially flexible, comfortable both in large groups or being alone. He does not have strong urge to move toward or away from people. His overall inclusion need strength is moderately high.

His low scores on control reflect that he generally avoids making decisions and taking responsibilities and most comfortable when others do not try to control them. Neither he is dependent nor he is inadequate but has doubts about their abilities to handle new areas of responsibilities, where he doesn't have prior experience. He will take charge of new areas of responsibilities in his own pace. He will normally not push others too much and avoid telling them what to do.

His affection score is high both in expressed and in wanted behavior. It reflects that he not only initiates warm and intimate relationships with others but also is very comfortable when others do that toward him. Since he seeks very high amount of affection from others, he may frequently get disappointed. However he is optimistic; hence, he will put efforts to get love and affection when his need is not getting satisfied.

Looking into a detailed analysis of FIRO-B, the coach will get an overall picture of the interpersonal need of this executive and may further explore the pros and cons of his interpersonal behaviors with the executive on the following areas:

1. Difference between expressed and wanted scores
2. Low scores on control
3. High scores on affection

Since, FIRO-B deals with the behavior of executive, the executive can identify what behavior he needs to change to improve his interpersonal effectiveness at his workplace, so that the corporate coach can facilitate the change process using behavioral coaching methodology.

Over the years, Schutz revised and expanded the FIRO theory and developed additional instruments. FIRO element B instrument, developed from FIRO-B, focuses on three interpersonal contents area—inclusion, control, and openness (affection in FIRO-B instrument). Element B measures expressed (what I do), received (what I receive), perceived (what I see), and wanted (what I want) behaviors. As a result, FIRO Element B gives 12 scores as compared to six scores of FIRO-B, as explained in Table 9.3.

FIRO Element B also calculates "Dissatisfaction" scores besides scores on 12 elements. Dissatisfaction scores are defined as "I don't

Table 9.3 FIRO Element B Scales

	Perceived (See)	Wanted (Want)
Expressed (Do) Inclusion	I include people	I want to include people
Expressed (Do) Control	I control people	I want to control people
Expressed (Do) Openness	I am open with people	I want to be open with people
Received (Get) Inclusion	People include me	I want people to include me
Received (Get) Control	People control me	I want people to control me
Received (Get) Openness	People are open with me	I want people to be open with me

have what I want"—the difference between the scores of "What I Want" and "What I Get." It may be interpreted in two ways:

1. *Unhappiness:* Let us look into one example. Let us assume the executive score on "People include me" is 3, whereas the score on "I want people to include me" is 8. This difference of 5 may be a source of great dissatisfaction in an executive's life and lead to unhappiness.
2. *Recognition:* Alternatively, this difference may simply be recognition of the state the executive is at the present. He may recognize that things are not the way he wants them to be.

In both the situations, the Dissatisfaction score opens a coaching opportunity for the executive and the coach can explore further, if any action is required.

Bar-On Emotional Quotient Inventory (EQ-i 2.0)

The Emotional Quotient Inventory (EQ-i 2.0) was developed by Dr Reuven Bar-On, a clinical psychologist, to assess emotional-social intelligence based on the EQ-i 2.0 model. The EQ-i is a self-report measure of emotionally and socially intelligent behavior that provides an estimate of emotional-social intelligence. In this model, emotional intelligence is defined as a set of emotional and social skills that collectively establish how well one perceives and expresses oneself, develops, and maintains social relationships, copes with challenges, and uses emotional information in an effective and meaningful way.

The EQ-i 2.0 inventory consists of 133 items in the form of short sentences and employs a 5-point response scale with a textual response format. It takes approximately 30 minutes to complete. It gives an overall EQ score as well as scores for the five composite scales and 15 subscales. Five composite scales are self-perception, self-expression, interpersonal, decision making, and stress management.

EQ-i 2.0 report also gives the well-being indicator, i.e., Happiness score, which is a reflection of feeling of satisfaction, contentment, and the ability to enjoy the many aspects of one's life. Annexure 9.1 gives one sample EQ-i 2.0 report.

Self-perception composite scale pertains to the assessment of the inner self, i.e., self-regard, self-actualization, and emotional self-awareness. Self-regard subscale indicates how accurately they perceive, understand, and accept themselves. It is extremely important for individuals to have confidence in their skills and abilities. Individuals who are assured of themselves generally have a positive outlook, are able to express themselves with confidence, and are happier in their life. They are aware of their strengths and weaknesses. Self-actualization is the willingness to persistently try to improve oneself and engage in the pursuits of personally relevant and meaningful objectives that lead to a rich and enjoyable life. Emotional Self-awareness indicates how much individuals are effective in recognizing and understanding their own feelings and emotions. Being aware of emotions is critical when interacting with others at the workplace and is essential to work performance.

Emotional expression, a subscale of Self-expression, reflects how openly one expresses one's feelings verbally and non-verbally. Assertiveness subscale measures the ability to express one's feelings, convictions, and opinions in a constructive manner. It is important for individuals to be able to express their ideas clearly and confidently to coworkers at the workplace. Independence measures the ability to be self-reliant and self-directed in one's thinking and actions as well as free of emotional dependence on others. Independence subscale measures the ability to be self-directed and free from emotional dependence from others. Decision-making, planning, and daily tasks are completed autonomously.

Interpersonal composite scale deals with the ability to develop and maintain relationships based on trust and compassion, articulate an understanding of another's perspective, and act responsibly while showing concerns for others. Interpersonal relationships subscale reflects the ability to develop and maintain mutually satisfying relationships that are characterized by trust and compassion. Empathy subcomponent measures an individual's ability to be aware of, understand, and appreciate how other people feel. Social responsibility subcomponent indicates how effectively any individual can identify one's social group and cooperate with other individuals or groups within the organization.

Decision-making scale reflects how well one understands the impacts emotions have on decision making, including the ability to resist or delay impulses and remains objective. Problem-solving subscale deals with how effectively personal and interpersonal problems are solved, where emotions are involved. Reality testing subscale deals with the validation of one's feelings and thinking with external realities objectively. Impulse control reflects the ability to resist or delay an impulse, drive or temptation to act, and involves rash behavior and decision making.

Stress management component consists of flexibility, stress tolerance, and optimism. Stress tolerance is defined as the ability to effectively manage one's emotions and the emotions of others in order to positively cope with stress. Flexibility subscale measures how one adopts and adjusts one's feelings and thinking to new situations. Optimism subscale measures the ability to maintain a positive attitude even when faced with adversity.

EQ-i 2.0 generates two reports, one for the executive, known as Workplace Report, and the other for Coach. The standard report begins with graphical display of the results of Total EI, the 5 composite scales and the 15 subscales, in three ranges, viz., low range, mid-range and high range. The average range score is 100 with standard deviation of 15. The total EI score indicates how effective they are in overall emotional and social functioning. EQ-i 2.0 norms are based on a sample of 4,000 people from North America, comprising equal representation of gender and age groups. Three types of norms, i.e., general population, age/gender, and professional norms, are available for EQ-i 2.0 inventory. In the balancing EI section of each subscale report, it gives the related subscale that has significant difference of 10 and more. In the coach report, it gives for three related subscales, whereas it is only the highest difference between that subscale and fifteen other subscales, presented with details of its implication in the executive report. In the coach report, additional information on responses of each item, response distribution, inconsistency index, and positive and negative impression are provided besides follow-up questions for each subscale.

EQ-i 2.0 assessment report is designed to provide the executive awareness with regard to their emotional and social functioning at work. Corporate coaches help the executive determine the areas that are critical and important for their job success. After identifying the developmental area(s), the coach supports the executive to develop strategies for behavioral change with a detailed action plan and how to acquire new behavior. EQ-i 2.0 report also suggests various developmental strategies for all subscales, so that executives can choose appropriate action based on their development needs.

DISC Instrument

DISC instrument is an instrument developed based on the theory of Dr William Marston. Dr Marston intended to explain how normal human emotions lead to differences in behavioral reactions among people to a particular work environment. It also addresses why there is a change in a person's behavior from time to time. DISC instrument measures the surface traits or characteristic ways of behaving in a particular situation, not to describe human characteristics that are not readily observable by others. He postulated a theory of human behavior as a function of two bipolar dimensions, one external and the other internal. The external environment can be described in terms of a continuum with opposing poles: antagonistic and favorable. The internal reaction of individuals can be described along a continuum from opposing poles, activity to passivity. These two dimensions provide a matrix from which the individual's typical pattern of interaction could be described through four characteristics—Dominance (D), Influence (I),

Steadiness (S), and Conscientiousness (C). He claimed that people would generally display one or more of these characteristics in the working environment.

Dominance: Dominance is the factor of directness, assertiveness, and control. People who score high on D are described as demanding, forceful, strong-willed, competitive, ambitious, determined, aggressive, independent-minded, motivated to succeed, and effective at getting their way. Low D people are described as cautious, mild, modest, peaceful, cooperative, conservative, undemanding, and low keyed. People who have D as prominent in their profile often try to maintain authority and power over others, and in general, on the environment they work. They seem to take challenges and rarely back away from difficult situations.

Influence: People with high I scores are described as influencing, friendly, extroverted, sociable, warm, and open to others. They are characterized as convincing, persuasive, trusting, optimistic, and demonstrative. They are guided more by their feelings, highly communicative, and socially confident. Person with low I are described as reflective, skeptical, calculative, critical, logical, and matter of fact person.

Steadiness: People who show a high level of S score are patient, undemanding, sympathetic listener, calm, relaxed, stable, consistent, persistent, and power of concentration allow them to work steadily.. They do not like sudden change but prefer to work in predictable and constant environment. People with low S score prefer to have change and variety. They are restless, demonstrative, impulsive, and impatient.

Compliance: People with high C score are structured, detailed oriented, systematic, cautious, adhere to rules and procedures, and display high level in precision and accuracy in their work. They would like to do quality work and do it right. Individuals with low S scores are described as unsystematic, stubborn, independent-minded, and may challenge established rules and procedures. In extremely difficult situations, people with high C scores delay actions till the last moment in order to find possible solutions.

DISC instrument forces respondents to choose the words most and the least describing himself or herself out of four choices in each of the 24 questions. By charting these choices scientifically, DISC instrument provides an insight into how this person copes with the environment and in turn gives a key to his/her present attitudes and possible performance.

It takes approximately 10–15 minutes to complete the instrument and the DISC profile is generated through software. Other most popular instruments based on the DISC theory are DISCUS, Thomas Profiling, DISC Classic, Personal Profile System, etc.

DISC instrument gives the DISC profile of the executive, which in fact gives the general characteristics of the work profile, their motivation, permanent traits, potential traits, transient traits, behavioral adaption, communication style, decision making, organization and planning, management style, etc., of the executive. Role Behavior analysis gives the behavioral competency required for the role, the executive is at present, or would like to move on. A comparison of DISC Role Behavior Analysis and DISC profile gives a list of the behavioral competencies that are to be developed or changed for the executive.

SPIRO-M Instrument

A person influences other persons with whom he/she interacts. In some roles, influence is a central function. One of the main functions of a role holder in an organization is to influence others for the achievement of work objectives. Those in influencing roles not only solve problems and help others, but also make an impact on others' ability to solve future problems. Another managerial function is to help one's subordinates to develop.

The Styles Profile of Interaction Roles in Organization for managers (SPIRO-M) instrument developed by Pareek (1997) to obtain a profile of managing styles—low or high frequency or intensity along specific dimensions. Each person involved in transactions with others has three ego states:

1. The Parent, which regulates behavior (through prescriptions and sanctions)
2. The Adult, which collects information and processes it
3. The Child, which is primarily concerned with (a) creativity, curiosity, (b) reactions to others, and (c) adjusting to others' demand

Each ego state is important in managerial role. The functional or dysfunctional roles of these ego states depend on the life position a manager takes. Harries(1969) has conceptualized four life positions: I'm OK-you're OK; I'm not OK-you're OK; I'm OK-You're not OK; and I'm not OK-You're not OK. James (1975) has suggested that, in general, the concepts of OK and not OK can be used to understand how managers behave. As James (1975) and Avery (1980) suggested, the six ego states can be combined with the two life positions (OK and not OK), hence there are 12 influencing styles (Table 9.4).

The SPIRO-M is a self-report instrument containing 36 statements. Responses are collected on a five-point scale. The SPIRO-M report gives the dominant and supporting influential styles, underdeveloped ego state, if any, and the operating effectiveness indices of six ego states, which show how effectively the OK dimension of a particular ego state is being used.

Table 9.4 Twelve Influence Styles

Ego States	Styles in Two Life Positions	
	Not OK	OK
Nurturing parent	Rescuing	Supportive
Regulating parent	Prescriptive	Normative
Adult	Task obsessive	Problem solving
Creative child	Innovative	Bohemian
Reactive child	Aggressive	Confronting
Adaptive child	Sulking	Resilient

Source: Pareek (1997).

The Operating Effectiveness Quotient (OEQ) of each ego style indicates how effectively the respondents are using that style in their managerial role. If the OK score is higher than the not-OK score on that style, it means that he is effective in that style. However, if the not-OK score is higher than the OK score, he is not effective on that style. OEQ is calculated using the formula: (OK − 3) × 100/(OK + not-OK − 6). Managers may show several of these behaviors mentioned above. However, they use one style more frequently than the others. If the dominant behavior is from OK dimension, then there will be higher effective interpersonal relationship in the coaching process. Let me explain through one example. One middle-level operation manager of a large corporation was administered this instrument. Based on his responses, it emerged that his regulating parent function has low OEQ, based on the norms. This reflects that he tends to prescribe his subordinated what he think should be done in order to establish norms. This resulted in his subordinates not developing self-regulating behavior and the norms are not followed, when he is not present at the workplace. The manager may do the following to improve his OEQ index of regulating parent function:

- Instead of giving clear instructions to his team on what should or should not be done (which is kind of imposing his norms on others), he should encourage his team to explore what should or should not be done, and why.

- Instead of prescribing standards or practices to be followed (which may be seen as imposition), he may evolve the objectives to be achieved with his team and then develop norms and practices that will help him achieve the objectives. He should encourage his team to self-regulate and self-monitor, review with them from time to time how things are progressing, and what can be done to promote effectiveness.

- Instead of admonishing his team members for not acting according to his instruction on most occasions, he may like to explore why they could not do so.

VIA Inventory of Strengths and Strength Finders

Seligman and Csikszentmihalyi (2000) quote that "the time has arrived for a positive psychology, our message is to remind our field that psychology is not just the study of pathology, weakness and damage; it is also the study of strength and virtue. Treatment is not just fixing what is broken; it is nurturing what is best." They further quote, "No longer do the dominant theories (psychological) view individual as a passive vessel responding to stimuli; rather, individuals are now seen as decision makers, with choices, preferences and the possibility of becoming masterful, efficacious ..."

Martin Seligman, Mihaly Csikszentmihalyi, and Ed Diener developed the foundation of positive psychology in early 2000. Martin Seligman suggested that we study what is right about people and explore what is best about human being, instead of focusing on human failures and shortcomings. Based on the work of Seligman, Values in Action Institute of Character (VIA), founded by Dr Neal H. Mayerson, D. Manuel, and Rhoda Mayerson Foundation, introduced VIA classification and VIA Inventory of Strengths Survey (IS), based on three years' research and input from scores of experts from various disciplines.

Peterson and Seligman (2004) developed a 240-item self-report questionnaire to assess 24 strengths of characters, each categorized within six virtues. Virtues are defined as "the core characteristics valued by moral philosophers and religious thinkers" where character strengths are "the psychological ingredients—i.e., processes and mechanism—that define the virtues" (Peterson and Seligman, 2004). Six virtues are "Wisdom and Knowledge," "Courage," "Humanity," "Justice," "Temperance," and "Transcendence."

VIA offers free survey report to those who would like to know their five "signature strengths," those strengths that are most core to who they are (for further details, please visit www.viame.org). VIA Me! Pathway (paid report) is 19+ page report providing a detailed description of each of the signature strengths, including benefits of the strengths and other information to help on how to apply strengths in life.

Besides this, the VIA PRO report offers an in-depth and detailed exploration of "signature strengths," a summary of what research evidences on each signature strengths, issues related to underuse and overuse of the signature strengths, and a look at the balance of strengths on a continuum of head/heart and self/others. It also gives recommendation for building each of the 24 strengths.

When the executive takes the assessment, the coach assists the executive on how to access their strengths. The strength inventory results help the executive to increase their self-efficacy, which leads them to work for challenging goals with enthusiasm and confidence. The coach guides the executives on how to use their strengths in achieving their goals during the action planning stage. Sometimes, the coach asks their executive how they have used their strengths in the past in their work life either in achieving their success or in removing obstacles, so that the executives get insights on how they can access their strengths.

StrengthsFinder 2.0 is another tool developed by Gallup by a team of researchers led by Donald O. Clifton. Gallup believed, based on their 40 years of study, that people have several times more potential for growth when they invest energy in developing their strengths instead of correcting their deficiencies. Initial assessment tool, known as Clifton Strengths Finder assessment, created a language of the 34 most common themes for talent. Strengths Finder actually is a measure of talent, not strengths. The 34 themes represent Gallup attempts at creating a common language or classification of talents. After completing the StrengthsFinder 2.0 assessment, the report gives the following:

1. Top five theme report, built around the Strengths Insight descriptions
2. Fifty ideas for action (ten for each of top five themes)
3. Strengths Discovery Interview to help on how experience, skills, and knowledge can be used to build strengths
4. A strength-based action plan

Readers can read more about this tool from the book of Tom Rath on StrengthsFinder 2.0, published by Gallup Press or website www.sf2.strengthsfinder.com.

Occupational Personality Questionnaire (OPQ/OPQ32)

The Occupational Personality Questionnaire (commonly referred to as "OPQ" or "OPQ32") was launched in 1984 by SHL (Saville and Holdsworth). It is a globally well-known tool extensively used in the selection, development, succession, and transition of potential and current executives/employees in both public and private sector organizations across a range of job levels. The OPQ32 model proposes that current and future behaviors are influenced by the personality of individuals and work groups. Reports from OPQ32 provide information on how dispositions are likely to influence the present or future manifestation of desired behaviors in a given organizational or role context. The dimensions assessed are centered upon three personality areas, namely the thinking domain, the relating domain, and the feeling domain. The thinking domain covers traits such as abstract thinking, and practical and detailed consciousness. The relating domain covers traits of social relationships. The feeling domain includes traits such as anxiety, tough-mindedness, and emotional control.

There is a normative version (OPQ32n) and an ipsative version (OPQ32i) of OPQ32. Both are designed to measure 32 facets of personality that are relevant to occupational uses such as selection, promotion, counseling, development, team building, organizational change and audits, training needs analysis, and research. The 32 facets of personality are grouped into three domains, further divided into subdomains. The three domains are relationships with people, thinking style, and feelings and emotions.

The newly launched OPQ32r is a significantly improved OPQ32 and revolutionized workplace personality assessment tool by using the latest techniques to make it faster, easier to use, more powerful, and more precise.

Sixteen Personality Factors (16 PF)

English-born US psychologist Raymond Cattell constructed the Sixteen Personality Factor (16 PF) instrument in early 1956. There are different definitions of personality defined by psychologists. However, Cattell mentioned that personality "... enables us to predict what a person will do in real life situations." Hence, Catell's 16 PF questionnaire is based on the assumption that personality is described by 16 traits, including dimensions such as outgoingness, social boldness, conscientiousness, tough-mindedness, and openness to change.

The 16 primary personality factors were derived by successive reductions, using factor analysis of 17,953 personality traits. The test has been refined and extended but has not changed fundamentally in nature. The personality factors measured by 16 PF instrument are not just unique to the test but rest within the context of a general personality theory. These are essentially independent.

The 16 PF questionnaire measures 16 primary bipolar dimensions of personality traits, named Factors A, B, C, E, F, G, H, I, L, M, N, O, Q1, Q2, Q3, and Q4. In addition to these, at least five second-order dimensions, which are broader traits, are calculated from the primary factor scores.

There are different versions of the 16 PF questionnaire, requiring 30–60 minutes for administration. The 16 PF answer sheet is scored manually using stencil or through computer. The raw scores are calculated from the responses to the questionnaire and then the raw score is converted to sten scores (the term comes from standard ten) using norm table available for a similar defined population. Computer scoring interpretive reports are being used more frequently to reduce errors and save time.

Multidimensional measures of personality are particularly helpful in the coaching relationship to build the executives' awareness of their preferred styles of thinking and behaving across situations. This kind of assessment can help explain why some people are well suited to some kinds of work environments or situations while others are not. It can also help explain why some situations or tasks are more stressful than others (Passmore, 2008).

Many researchers felt that Catell's theory was too complex. As a result, the big five-factor theory evolved to describe the basic traits that serve as the building block of personality. Measures of the five-factor model of personality are based on the accepted premise that all personality attributes are represented in five core, broadband attributes, commonly referred to as the "Big five" (Goldberg,1990). While there is a significant body of literature supporting this five-factor model of personality, researchers do not always agree on the exact labels for each dimension. However, these five categories are usually described as follows:

1. *Extraversion:* This trait includes characteristics such as excitability, fun loving, friendly, sociability, talkativeness, assertiveness, and high amounts of emotional expressiveness.
2. *Agreeableness:* This personality dimension includes attributes such as trust, altruism, kindness, affection, flexible, generous, and other pro-social behaviors.
3. *Conscientiousness*: Common features of this dimension include high levels of thoughtfulness, careful, reliable, with good impulse control, and goal-directed behaviors. Those high in conscientiousness tend to be organized and mindful of details.
4. *Emotional stability:* Individuals high in this trait tend to experience emotional instability, anxiety, moodiness, irritability, and sadness.
5. *Openness to experience*: This trait features characteristics such as original, creative, curious, imagination and insight, and those high in this trait also tend to have a broad range of interests.

It is important to note that each of the five personality factors represents a range between two extremes. For example, extraversion represents a continuum between extreme extraversion and extreme introversion. In the real world, most people lie somewhere in between the two polar ends of each dimension.

Chapter Summary

Corporate coach uses a wide range of psychological tools and inventories, having tested for psychometric properties, in coaching for creating self-awareness of the executive, in order to help them to understand who they are, what gifts they have, what strengths they can leverage on, and what are the preferred styles and preferences so that they can pursue their developmental journey with better awareness on self. Though there are a variety of tools available in the market, it is advisable to check reliability and validity data of individual tests as well as refer the appropriate norm, applicable to the executive undergoing coaching.

The Myers-Briggs Type Indicator (MBTI) tool provides a categorization of personality typology into sixteen different types, reflecting on broad differences in attitudes and orientations. Each type defines a specific set of behavioral tendencies, due to basic differences the way individual prefers to use their perception and judgment. Sixteen personality Factor (16 PF) is a multi-dimensional measurement of personality. Big Five Factor personality assessment is based on the premise that all personality attributes are represented in five broad factors of personality. These are Conscientiousness, Extroversion, Agreeableness, Emotional Stability, and Openness to Experience. The Occupational Personality Questionnaire (OPQ) 32 model proposes that the current and future work behavior is influenced by the personality of individuals.

Values in Action (VIA) inventory and Strength Finders are two important coaching instruments for coaches who have strong conviction on positive psychology. These two inventories allow the executives to develop their awareness on their strengths so that they can leverage it for their growth.

The FIRO-B inventory measures interpersonal relationship orientation of individuals, which allows predicting their interpersonal behavior at the workplace and helps executives to understand self vis-à-vis in developing healthy relationship. DISC predicts the behavior of individual at the workplace based on specific characteristics displayed by them. EQ-i 2.0 measures emotional and social intelligence in five composite scales and fifteen subscales, which ultimately impact the leadership competencies.

Finally, each tool mentioned in this chapter has specific use in the coaching context. Hence, corporate coaches take conscious decision on which tool is appropriate for the context of the executive, their developmental agenda based on a proper understanding of interpreting the results.

Annexure 9.1: Overview of EQ-i 2.0 Result

		70	90	110	130

Total EI — 108

Self-Perception Composite — 102
Self-Regard — 101
Self-Actualization — 105
Emotional Self-Awareness — 100

Self-Expression Composite — 112
Emotional Expression — 111
Assertiveness — 102
Independence — 116

Interpersonal Composite — 108
Interpersonal Relationships — 98
Empathy — 112
Social Responsibility — 111

Decision-Making Composite — 109
Problem Solving — 110
Impulse Control — 104
Reality Testing — 107

Stress Management Composite — 102
Flexibility — 99
Stress Tolerance — 103
Optimism — 104

70	90	110	130
Low Range	Mid-Range	High Range	

References

Avery, B. (1980). Ego states: Manifestation of psychic organs. *Transactional Analysis Journal*, 10 (4), pp. 291–294.

Goldberg, L.R. (1990). An alternative 'description of personality': A big-five factor structure. *Journal of Personality and Social Psychology*, 59, pp. 1216–1229.

James, M. (1975). *The OK boss*. Reading, Massachusetts: Addison-Wesley.

Myers, I.B., McCaully, M.H., Quenk, N.L., & Hammer, A.L. (1998). *MBTI manual: A guide to the development and use of the myers-briggs type indicator*, 3rd ed. California: Consulting Psychologists Press, Inc.

The Occupational Personality Questionnaire, www.shl.com/assests/resources/opq-uk.pdf accessed on October 1, 2013.

Pareek, U. (1997). *Training instruments for human resource development*. New Delhi: Tata Mcgraw-Hill Publishing.

Passmore, J. (2008). *Psychometrics in coaching, using psychological and psychometric tools for development*. London: Kogen Page.

Peterson, C. & Seligman, M.E.P. (2004). *Character strengths and virtues: A handbook and classification*. Washington, D.C.: American Psychological Association.

Schutz, W. (1958). *FIRO: A three-dimensional theory of interpersonal behavior*. New York: Rinehart.

Seligman, M. & Csikszentmihalyi, M. (2000). Positive psychology: An introduction. *American Psychologists*, 55 (1), pp. 5–14.

CHAPTER 10

360-Degree Survey in Coaching Need Assessment

One tool that has predominantly gained popularity in corporations of India is 360-degree feedback survey. This is because organizational leaders realized that it is necessary to get multiple perspectives, instead of single assessment of reporting officer, for objective evaluation of competencies (mostly soft skills) of employees, which ultimately lead to performance. Though the 360-degree feedback survey is not a new tool, many organizations conduct yearly 360-degree feedback survey for their employees as a part of their performance and development management program. Organizations feel that 360-degree feedback survey is a very useful tool for identifying developmental needs of their executives. Many Fortune 500 companies world over and large corporations in India are using 360-degree evaluation in one form or the other.

360-Degree feedback survey is a formalized and structured process whereby an employee receives feedback on his performance, competencies, and behavior from multiple individuals or raters, who regularly interact with the executive as well as self-assessment by the executive/employee. The raters typically represent the executive/employee's boss, peers, subordinates, customers, or suppliers who are credible and familiar with the executive's working. 360-degree feedback generally measures "How" not "What," i.e., the focus is on process rather than on content. In corporate coaching domain,

360-feedback survey is being used as the starting point of corporate coaching journey.

The purpose of conducting 360-degree feedback survey is to provide their employees with feedback on their performance, behaviors, and skills and their potential as observed by the raters, so that the executive gets an opportunity to understand and improve any gap or issues that may exist between his performance, skill, competency, or behavior as perceived by themselves and other stakeholders in the organization.

Broadly, 360-degree feedback survey does the following things:

1. It provides multi-source, multi-rater objective assessment of the executive's competencies (knowledge, skills, and behavior), working styles, personal qualities, and its impact on others.
2. It provides feedback that is more acceptable to the executive.
3. It reduces individual biases, which are very common in single-rater assessment, such as performance appraisal.
4. It includes feedback from external stakeholders, such as customers, suppliers, etc. Self-appraisal is also an important component of 360-degree feedback survey.
5. It provides insight of strong and weak areas of the executive. Identification of the development needs for the executive is crucial for executive's performance and growth. Leveraging on the area of strength helps executives to further improve their performance.
6. It provides an opportunity for developmental planning for the executive.

360-Degree feedback survey is highly effective if the organization culture is conducive for such intervention and a high amount of preparatory work is undertaken before introduction. If there is no cohesiveness, trust, and respect among employees, it may happen that the raters may not give their opinion honestly or they may form a collusion of rating each other high or develop retaliatory behavior toward others. In those situations, 360-degree feedback survey is not an appropriate tool for the organizations.

While introducing the 360-degree assessment for coaching, the following broad steps are undertaken:

Preparation stage: The most important questions of any 360-degree evaluation are what are the criteria on which evaluation needs to be done and whether to use standardized, packaged assessment tool available in the marketplace or not. There are many standard and validated 360 assessment tools available in the market, and each tool measures specific sets of skills, behaviors, and competencies. The most commonly used tools in coaching are EQ360, LSI (life-styles inventory), Campbell leadership index, Benchmark, Hogan Development Survey, etc. Using standardized tool is always prefer-able than developing new tools, since all standardized tools are tested for psychometric properties and norms are available. Moreover, each standardized tool gives comprehensive analysis of results as well as broad developmental planning guidelines.

The limitations of standardized tools are that each tool evaluates specific sets of behaviors or competencies, which may not be aligned with the unique competencies of the organization or the competen-cies required for the position holders to achieve the organizational goals and strategies. In some situations, organization may decide specific developmental areas the executives need to strengthen for their existing role or future roles, which may not be covered in the off-the-self assessment tools. Most of the standard assessment tools give quantitative evaluations (e.g., 1–5 or 1–10 scale) but focus less on behavioral issues. A good 360-degree feedback questionnaire should include the behaviors, skills, and competencies that are rel-evant for the executive and the raters are able to choose responses based on what behaviors the raters actually observed or noticed the application of such behavior rather than guessing it.

If the 360-degree feedback questionnaire is designed based on the organizational requirements or on specific coaching requirements, then the questionnaire is required to be pre-tested for reliability and validity within a small representative sample. A sample 360-degree feedback survey designed and administered for the leadership team at a manufacturing-based organization by the author is given in Annexure 10.1 for reference.

While designing the questionnaire, it is important to keep in mind that there is enough opportunity for raters to justify their ratings with evidences, which ultimately help the executive at a later stage in interpretation of the results. After finalizing the instrument, the next step is to identify the raters. Normally, the coach, the executive, and the representative from the human resource department jointly decide 8–10 raters from superior officers, peers, subordinates, customers, or vendors, having at least 3 from each group of raters, except for the superior category. Sometimes, it is difficult to find 8–10 raters who know the individual well enough to give insightful feedback. It is may be due to frequent organizational changes or the rater identified may have not worked with him for a considerable period of time or some rater may be new to the organization. It is important that all the identified raters necessarily interact with the executive/employee for a minimum six months. Another problem arises when one rater is rating many individuals, then after one or two feedbacks, the attitude of the rater becomes just completing the work within the time constraints, not giving enough thoughts in each feedback. In that situation, care is taken that any rater should not rate more than three ratees in a short period of time, say within a week.

After identifying the raters, organization sends communication to all the raters explaining the objectives and purposes of this exercise, what is expected from them, and how much their honest and objective inputs are important in this process. Some organizations conduct training sessions or communication meeting for all the raters, so that they get familiarized on the process, which in turn gets all the raters enrolled in the exercise.

Administration stage: Organizations then decide when to start the evaluation, the time period during which the data are to be collected, who will be the process owner, and the mode of administration of the survey. With easy availability of technology, most of the 360-degree feedback surveys nowadays are administered online to keep the feedback confidential, to cover a large number of executives/employees working at various locations, and to make the analysis simpler.

Analysis stage: If standardized test is administered, then comprehensive analysis is available to the coach and the executive. If the instrument is designed by the coach, then the coach decides what are the analysis to be done, how the data are to be presented, what sort of comparisons are to be incorporated, how the qualitative and behavioral data are to be compiled, etc. The feedback survey report generally contains a brief on how to read the report, developmental planning work-sheet, and guidelines for further actions. Figure 10.1 gives a snapshot of summary of 360-degree feedback survey result. Annexure 10.2 gives an example of a part of the detailed feedback report.

Figure 10.1 A Sample of Overall Score Overview

Feedback stage: This is the most sensitive stage in 360-degree feedback for the executive. The coach helps the executive on how to read the report in the right perspectives so that the executive is able to identify his developmental needs. In some cases, the feedback affirms the areas the executives are aware of themselves as well as matches with their perceptions, but it will also identify a few areas that need their immediate attention. In some cases, the feedback report may be hard-hitting, a total surprise for the executive and may even be de-motivating. Here the coach assists the executives to examine the feedback from their work perspectives and their work context so that they can identify if there are any clear messages that they agree on or disagree with. Debriefing 360-degree feedback to the executive is a skill. Corporate coaches are generally trained on how to debrief the feedback survey results to coaching executives.

Debriefing is done based on the 3A's model of change: Awareness, Acceptance, and Action. First one or two sessions of debriefing is primarily focused on creating an awareness of assessment tools, its assumptions, what it measures, its limitations, etc. After creating awareness on the 360-degree assessment tool, the coach assists the executive to create an understanding of what are the results of the survey, i.e., what are the messages for him. While going through the feedback results, the executive may experience surprise, confusion, dissonance, denial, or rejection. Hence it requires time for the executive to accept the feedback by reflecting on it over a period of time. So the coach requests the executive to reflect on the results till the next coaching session. After a gap of 15 days to one month, the action stage comes when the executive has got time to interpret the results in his own perspectives and accept the feedback to a reasonable extent.

The coach may ask the executive to do the following in the acceptance phase, while reading the report:

1. Identify three to four areas of strengths based on the ratings received from all the raters.
2. Identify three to four areas of development based on ratings received.

3. Identify three to four areas where there are major gaps between self-rating and overall ratings from raters.
4. Identify three to four areas that surprised him/her, whether it is his/her strength areas or areas of development.
5. Identify areas where there are major differences in ratings of different rater groups.

It is not necessary for the executive to agree with the feedback report completely. The objective of debriefing is the executive should be able to identify key strengths she/he possesses, key developmental opportunities, and the areas where there is major perception gap of his/her own assessment vis-à-vis others, as a whole or a group of raters, viz., peers, bosses, subordinates, etc. The coach assists the executive to examine the perception gaps and helps the executive explore why there is a major perception gap. The coaches are trained on how to analyze the data and how to present feedback to the executive/ employee, so that the ultimate objectives of 360-degree feedback are achieved. The coach encourages the executive/employee to reflect on the common themes or messages that the raters are making vis-à-vis their own self-assessment. When the executive/employee observes a consistent pattern in feedback from different sources, the executive/employee finds the feedback as important for his growth and effectiveness. When executives/employees accept the message from the feedback, there is a high possibility that they would like to undertake behavior change or improve skills.

The coach sometimes encourages the executive to do the following:

1. Go back to the people who participated and thank them for their inputs and time. This is because these people gave their time, thoughts, and inputs, which are important for his/her growth.
2. Tell the people one or two things she/he learned from 360-degree feedback results, which are important for him/her.
3. Tell the people what are their plans and in what way they can help or support him/her.

Developmental action planning: In the developmental planning stage, the coach suggests the executive to focus on the following, while selecting the developmental areas:

1. Identification of one strength area to capitalize on
2. Identification of one mid-range area of development, which needs to be made stronger
3. Identification of one development area having the lowest score

The coach then helps the executive define developmental goal for each area so that the detailed action plan can be developed to achieve the developmental goal. While developing the action plan, the executives also identify the resources they may need and what could be the obstacles. A specimen action planning sheet, given in Annexure 10.3, can be used for developmental planning.

Finally, giving feedback to the executive/employee is not a simple task. While positive feedback helps the executive/employee to reinforce behavior and higher motivation, negative impact of the feedback can be observed when the executive/employee displays behavior of withdrawal, defensiveness, mistrust, and a decreased level of commitment to change, or even in coaching. Sometime, 360-degree feedback can be damaging to some executives/employees, if the coach does not handle it properly. They may lose self-esteem, their egos may be hurt, their self-efficacy may reduce, or it may impact them emotionally.

The two most commonly used 360-degree feedback tools in corporate coaching are briefly discussed below.

Life Styles Inventory

The Life Styles Inventory (LSI), a 360-degree feedback tool, was developed by clinical psychologist Dr J. Clayton Lafferty, founder of Human Synergistic International during the early 1970s. The LSI assesses and provides feedback on thinking and behavioral patterns that people can change to develop themselves along multiple dimensions, including their ability to understand and manage their emotions.

Lafferty postulated that individuals' self-images are shaped by their patterns of thinking, including their perceptions about how others see them, their own self-image, and their perceptions of what they are vis-à-vis what they should be. Those who have a positive self-image will have a healthy relationship with others and strive toward self-actualization by realizing and exploiting their true potential. However, those who have an unhealthy interpersonal relationship with others have unrealistic expectations of what they should be and self-defeating beliefs about themselves create a negative self-image, resulting in underutilization of their potential. LSI, therefore, helps individuals in monitoring and modifying their personal thinking styles for growth, development and realization of their true potential.

The LSI measures personal orientations toward different thinking and behavioral styles based on one's needs and interests. It measures twelve distinct thinking and behavioral styles that are distinguished by their orientations toward task versus people and higher-order needs for satisfaction and growth versus lower needs for security and safety. The 12 Personal Managerial or Leadership Styles are as follows:

1. *Humanistic-encouraging (1 o'clock):* People with humanistic-encouraging style are interested in growth and development of people and have a high positive regard for others. They are empathetic, compassionate, thoughtful, considerate, and encourage others.
2. *Affiliative (2 o'clock):* People with affiliative style are friendly and cooperative with others. They are interested in developing sustainable relationship with others and make others feel as a part of them. They like people and enjoy people's interaction.
3. *Approval (3 o'clock):* The approval style reflects a need to be accepted by others. They try hard to please others, be

agreeable, and obedient. Fear of rejection limits them to confront others assumptions, thinking, and actions. Their self-efficacy is dependent on other's acceptance of them.

4. *Conventional (4 o'clock):* People high on this style prefer to follow established rules, procedures, and systems, like status quo and prefer a stable, predictable work environment. They are conformists, follow tried and tested techniques rather than trying new things, and lack flexibility and creativity in general.

5. *Dependent (5 o'clock):* People high on this style have a need of others to take charge of the situations, to make decisions for them, depend on others to help them in every occasion, since they have a belief that they do not have direct control over events or actions and they cannot make difference to others.

6. *Avoidance (6 o'clock):* People high on this style have a strong apprehension, a need for self-protection, "play it safe" attitude, and shy away from group activities. They lack true emotional and psychological engagement with others, because of fear of disapproval from others.

7. *Oppositional (7 o'clock):* Oppositional style reflects a strong need of security that is manifested in tough questioning, critical and cynical, at times. They ask questions to others, blame others for their own mistake, use criticism to gain attention of others, and are judgmental of others. Their behavior generally erodes relationship and trust.

8. *Power (8 o'clock):* This style reflects a need to control and influence others. They generally dictate other actions, try to do every activity by themselves, and treat others in aggressive and forceful manners.

9. *Competitive (9 o'clock):* People high on this scale motivate and drive others to operate in a win–lose situation, outperform their peers, and do anything necessary to look good.

10. *Perfectionist (10 o'clock):* This style reflects a need to set unrealistically high goals, stay on top of every detail, and work long hours to attain narrowly defined objectives.

11. *Achievement (11 o'clock):* People high on this scale motivate and encourage others to set challenging but realistic goals, establish plans to reach those goals, and pursue them with enthusiasm.

12. *Self-actualizing (12 o'clock):* This style reflects a need to gain enjoyment from their work, develop them professionally, and approach problems with interest, creativity, and integrity.

These 12 thinking and behavioral styles are organized into three general clusters:

1. *Constructive styles*: Achievement, self-actualizing, affiliative, and humanistic–encouraging.
2. *Passive/defensive styles*: Approval, conventional, dependent, and avoidance.
3. *Aggressive/defensive styles*: Oppositional, power, competitive, and perfectionistic.

The LSI comprises two inventories: LSI 1 and LSI 2. The LSI 1 is a self-assessment inventory of one's thinking styles and self-concept. The LSI 2 is completed by other associates up to 12 in number to get their perceptions about the individual. Both the inventories have 240 items and responses are collected in the following three options:

2: Like me/this person most of the time
1: Like me/this person quite often
0: Essentially unlike me/this person

Results are plotted in the Circumplex model of Dr Laffery, which is normed against 14,000 individuals (the details of the model can be viewed at : www.human-synergistics.com). The raw scores are converted into percentile or normed scores. There are five concentric circles on the profile representing the 10th, 25th, 50th, 75th, and 99th percentiles.

EQ 360 Assessment Tool

EQ 360 assessment tool is based on the EQ-i 2.0 model described earlier in the coaching instrument chapter. It measures the emotional and social skills of the EQ-i 2.0 model from various perspectives:

1. His or her self-perspective
2. His or her reporting manager's perspective
3. His or her direct report's perspective
4. His or her peer's perspective
5. Where appropriate, his or her friend's and family's, customers', executives' perspective, etc.

While selecting raters for this assessment, the ratee chooses the raters broadly based on the following criteria, so that an overall picture of the ratee can be obtained from a variety of raters:

1. A mix of people including those who know the ratee for a long time and those who know for a less time
2. Those who know the ratee well and those who know the ratee less well
3. Raters who trust the ratee and do not feel pressured into responding in a given way

There should be minimum three raters in each rater group except in the Manager group. If there is less than three raters in any category, then it is clubbed into "Other" category.

EQ 360 feedback assessment has the same 133 questions as in EQ-i 2.0, only the language of questions is changed for the raters. There is an option to choose up to five open-ended questions from the database or the test administrators can create their own. All verbatim responses of these open-ended questions are listed by the rater group, e.g., Direct Report 1, Direct Report 2, etc.

The report provides details of how many raters in each group responded as well as the details of responses for the following questions:

1. How long the rater has known the ratee being assessed?
2. How often the rater interacted with the ratee?
3. How well she/he knows the ratee being assessed?

The responses are normed against 3,200 samples, based on overall population, gender, and rater type, i.e., direct report, peers, etc. The report gives a summary report of five composite scales, overall EI, and fifteen subscales as rated by the executive as well as ratings given by different categories of raters. If the difference between self-rating and rating by any category of raters is more than 10, then "*" is marked against the score.

The profile gap analysis of the report gives a visual representation of an individual's self-rating in the y-axis and the level of agreement between the self-report and the other raters in the x-axis. Any subscale appearing in the "allied strength" quadrant represents that the self-rating is above 100 and the rater groups are in agreement with this score. Any subscale appearing in the reinforced opportunities reveals that the ratee has rated self as low and that the rater groups are in the agreement with the self-rating of the ratee. It means that there is a developmental need of the rate in this subscale and the self-perception has been confirmed by the other raters. Any subscale appearing in the right lower quadrant reflects that there is "Disconnect," meaning the self-assessment score is less than 100, whereas other raters do not agree with the self-rating score. The subscale appearing in the blind spot reflects that there is a gap between how the ratee sees himself or herself and how others see him or her.

Subscale pages of the report also highlights the gaps in each area where there is at least a 10 point difference between self-rating and a particular rater group rating. The closer agreement text is provided only if there is less than a 10-point gap between self-rating and rating of a specific rater group. It also provides one related subscale having the largest difference in Balancing EI section. However, in the coach report three related subscales comparisons are provided. In the coach report, follow-up questions for each subscale are also provided.

Chapter Summary

360-Degree assessment tool is an important tool for the coach, if it is effectively used to collect data for the executive from the raters. If raters do not participate in the process honestly and give objective assessment, a little will be gained from the exercise. While undertaking 360-degree assessment in coaching, a conscious decision is made whether to use standardized off-the-shelf tool or to design assessment tool based on specific organizational needs. Selection of raters, articulation within the organization, the purpose of undertaking 360 assessment tool, and planning before introduction of assessment are critical for obtaining meaningful input for the executive to identify their developmental needs. The role of the coach is to assist the executive/employee in interpreting the feedback report and to assist the executive/employee in identifying areas to be developed, so that an effective developmental plan can be developed.

Annexure 10.1: Sample 360-Degree Feedback Tool

360-degree feedback for:

Please give your feedback as (Please ☑ in the appropriate box.)

Self	
Superior	
Peer	
Subordinate	

Instructions:

1. The questionnaire is divided in two parts.

   - Part I: Based on your own experience, you are requested to indicate the extent to which you agree or disagree with the given statements, which are accurate descriptions of the executive. Only if you believe, you do not have enough experience or information to respond to a particular statement, choose the "N/A" to indicate "no opinion/insufficient information to reply." However this option shall be opted only as an exception.
   - Part II: You are requested to specify your suggestions on the executive's leadership style/trait.

2. The questionnaire will take approximately 30 minutes to complete.
3. Your frank and honest feedback will be extremely valuable to the concerned individual for his/her self-development. Please give your spontaneous, natural, and truthful responses.

Feedback PART–I:

No.	Statement	Your response (Pls. ☑ the appropriate box)		
I. MEETING ORGANIZATIONAL CHALLENGES				
I.a. Values and Integrity				
1	Practices group values and encourages subordinates to follow the same at all times.	Strongly Disagree ☐ ☐ ☐ ☐	Strongly Agree ☐ ☐	N/A ☐
2	Respects individual differences of others, treats people at all levels with dignity, respect, and fairness.	Strongly Disagree ☐ ☐ ☐ ☐	Strongly Agree ☐ ☐	N/A ☐
3	Strongly believes that customers/ vendors/distributors and the society at large are all important stakeholders for the overall growth and prosperity of the business.	Strongly Disagree ☐ ☐ ☐ ☐	Strongly Agree ☐ ☐	N/A ☐
4	Maintains unequivocal commitment to honesty/truth in every facet of behavior.	Strongly Disagree ☐ ☐ ☐ ☐	Strongly Agree ☐ ☐	N/A ☐
5	Fulfills all commitments; assumes responsibility for own mistakes.	Strongly Disagree ☐ ☐ ☐ ☐	Strongly Agree ☐ ☐	N/A ☐
6	Actions and behaviors are consistent with words. Absolutely trusted by others.	Strongly Disagree ☐ ☐ ☐ ☐	Strongly Agree ☐ ☐	N/A ☐
7	Leads by example; Walks the Talk.	Strongly Disagree ☐ ☐ ☐ ☐	Strongly Agree ☐ ☐	N/A ☐
8	Is a leader rather than a manager.	Strongly Disagree ☐ ☐ ☐ ☐	Strongly Agree ☐ ☐	N/A ☐

I.b. Organizational Objectives, Goals, and Strategy			
9	Understands higher management expectations, how higher management operates and how they see things.	Strongly Disagree ☐ ☐ ☐ ☐ Strongly Agree ☐ ☐	N/A ☐
10	Sets realistic goals and creates buy-in.	Strongly Disagree ☐ ☐ ☐ ☐ Strongly Agree ☐ ☐	N/A ☐
11	Makes sure employees have a clear understanding of the organization's goals.	Strongly Disagree ☐ ☐ ☐ ☐ Strongly Agree ☐ ☐	N/A ☐
12	Does whatever it takes to get things done despite resistance from important people inside/outside the organization.	Strongly Disagree ☐ ☐ ☐ ☐ Strongly Agree ☐ ☐	N/A ☐
13	Gets people to question their current approach constantly.	Strongly Disagree ☐ ☐ ☐ ☐ Strongly Agree ☐ ☐	N/A ☐
14	Undertakes challenging goals that contribute to profit maximization.	Strongly Disagree ☐ ☐ ☐ ☐ Strongly Agree ☐ ☐	N/A ☐
15	Ensures that financial targets are met.	Strongly Disagree ☐ ☐ ☐ ☐ Strongly Agree ☐ ☐	N/A ☐
I.c. Process Excellence and Continuous Improvement			
16	Is able to benchmark the existing process against the best in class.	Strongly Disagree ☐ ☐ ☐ ☐ Strongly Agree ☐ ☐	N/A ☐
17	Designs, implements, & promotes various strategies/practices for achieving process excellence.	Strongly Disagree ☐ ☐ ☐ ☐ Strongly Agree ☐ ☐	N/A ☐

18	Tries different and novel ways to deal with work problems & opportunities and encourages others to find out innovative ways to come out of the present problems.	Strongly Disagree ☐ ☐ ☐ ☐ Strongly Agree ☐ ☐	N/A ☐
19	Drives continuous improvement over previous levels.	Strongly Disagree ☐ ☐ ☐ ☐ Strongly Agree ☐ ☐	N/A ☐
20	Manages higher output with the same resources.	Strongly Disagree ☐ ☐ ☐ ☐ Strongly Agree ☐ ☐	N/A ☐
21	Reduces response and lead-time through work efficiency.	Strongly Disagree ☐ ☐ ☐ ☐ Strongly Agree ☐ ☐	N/A ☐

I.d. Innovation and Change Management

22	Drives innovation as a way of life.	Strongly Disagree ☐ ☐ ☐ ☐ Strongly Agree ☐ ☐	N/A ☐
23	Reinforces change by embracing it (prevent relapse into prior state).	Strongly Disagree ☐ ☐ ☐ ☐ Strongly Agree ☐ ☐	N/A ☐
24	Adjusts management style to changing situations	Strongly Disagree ☐ ☐ ☐ ☐ Strongly Agree ☐ ☐	N/A ☐
25	Implements new ideas generated from the shop floor.	Strongly Disagree ☐ ☐ ☐ ☐ Strongly Agree ☐ ☐	N/A ☐
26	Effectively involves key people in the design and implementation of change.	Strongly Disagree ☐ ☐ ☐ ☐ Strongly Agree ☐ ☐	N/A ☐
27	Creates learning culture in his/her function/department.	Strongly Disagree ☐ ☐ ☐ ☐ Strongly Agree ☐ ☐	N/A ☐

I.e. Quality Focus and Cost Management		
28	Able to demonstrate the organizational quality policy in practice at every step.	Strongly Disagree ☐ ☐ ☐ ☐ ☐ ☐ Strongly Agree N/A ☐
29	Maintains a thrust on continuous improvement of quality and process	Strongly Disagree ☐ ☐ ☐ ☐ ☐ ☐ Strongly Agree N/A ☐
30	Realistically assesses time and resources required to meet quality and performance targets	Strongly Disagree ☐ ☐ ☐ ☐ ☐ ☐ Strongly Agree N/A ☐
31	Creates a cost-effective environment in his/her function/department and motivates others to think in a cost-effective manner.	Strongly Disagree ☐ ☐ ☐ ☐ ☐ ☐ Strongly Agree N/A ☐
32	Continuously pursue cost compression practices and encourage others to save cost at every activity of operation	Strongly Disagree ☐ ☐ ☐ ☐ ☐ ☐ Strongly Agree N/A ☐

II. LEADING AND MANAGING PEOPLE

II.a. Communication/Influence

33	Communicates in open, candid, clear, complete, and consistent manner—invites response/dissent.	Strongly Disagree ☐ ☐ ☐ ☐ ☐ ☐ Strongly Agree N/A ☐
34	Communicates critical job task expectations and measurement standards clearly.	Strongly Disagree ☐ ☐ ☐ ☐ ☐ ☐ Strongly Agree N/A ☐
35	Uses facts and rational arguments to influence and persuade.	Strongly Disagree ☐ ☐ ☐ ☐ ☐ ☐ Strongly Agree N/A ☐
36	Is open to the input of others.	Strongly Disagree ☐ ☐ ☐ ☐ ☐ ☐ Strongly Agree N/A ☐

37	Open-minded & receptive to feedback about himself/herself.	Strongly Disagree ☐ ☐ ☐ ☐ Strongly Agree ☐ ☐	N/A ☐
38	Provides timely guidance & feedback to help employees, clarifies expected behaviors, knowledge, and level of proficiency by seeking and giving information.	Strongly Disagree ☐ ☐ ☐ ☐ Strongly Agree ☐ ☐	N/A ☐

II.b. Team-Building and Interpersonal Relationship

39	Delegates tasks; empowers team to maximize effectiveness. Is personally a team player.	Strongly Disagree ☐ ☐ ☐ ☐ Strongly Agree ☐ ☐	N/A ☐
40	When working with a group over whom he/she has no control, gets thing done by finding common ground.	Strongly Disagree ☐ ☐ ☐ ☐ Strongly Agree ☐ ☐	N/A ☐
41	Can settle problems with external groups without alienating them.	Strongly Disagree ☐ ☐ ☐ ☐ Strongly Agree ☐ ☐	N/A ☐
42	Promotes inter-departmental understanding.	Strongly Disagree ☐ ☐ ☐ ☐ Strongly Agree ☐ ☐	N/A ☐
43	Has the ability to create a team environment based on mutual respect and trust.	Strongly Disagree ☐ ☐ ☐ ☐ Strongly Agree ☐ ☐	N/A ☐
44	Manages conflicts among team members effectively.	Strongly Disagree ☐ ☐ ☐ ☐ Strongly Agree ☐ ☐	N/A ☐

II.c. People Management

45	Demonstrates caring for people.	Strongly Disagree ☐ ☐ ☐ ☐ Strongly Agree ☐ ☐	N/A ☐

46	Ensures that employees' development is a sustained initiative and not a one-off exercise.	Strongly Disagree ☐ ☐ ☐ ☐ ☐ ☐ Strongly Agree	N/A ☐
47	Gives people the space & freedom to work (avoidance of micro-management).	Strongly Disagree ☐ ☐ ☐ ☐ ☐ ☐ Strongly Agree	N/A ☐
48	Shares credit for success and takes accountability for failures.	Strongly Disagree ☐ ☐ ☐ ☐ ☐ ☐ Strongly Agree	N/A ☐
49	Sensitive to the need for balance between people's personal and professional lives.	Strongly Disagree ☐ ☐ ☐ ☐ ☐ ☐ Strongly Agree	N/A ☐
50	Is straightforward with individuals about consequences and expected action or decision.	Strongly Disagree ☐ ☐ ☐ ☐ ☐ ☐ Strongly Agree	N/A ☐

II.d. Performance Orientation

51	Monitors performance of subordinates against agreed targets and encourages them to take corrective actions.	Strongly Disagree ☐ ☐ ☐ ☐ ☐ ☐ Strongly Agree	N/A ☐
52	Proactively ensures that people improve their performance.	Strongly Disagree ☐ ☐ ☐ ☐ ☐ ☐ Strongly Agree	N/A ☐
53	Facilitates people to perform as per role expectation.	Strongly Disagree ☐ ☐ ☐ ☐ ☐ ☐ Strongly Agree	N/A ☐
54	Recognizes people's performance achievement when they do well.	Strongly Disagree ☐ ☐ ☐ ☐ ☐ ☐ Strongly Agree	N/A ☐

III. CUSTOMER ORIENTATION

55	Drives a customer-centric culture in the organization.	Strongly Disagree ☐ ☐ ☐ ☐ ☐ ☐ Strongly Agree	N/A ☐

56	Listens to customers and assigns the highest priority to customer satisfaction, including internal customers.	Strongly Disagree ☐ ☐ ☐ ☐ ☐ ☐	Strongly Agree	N/A ☐
57	Personally keeps in touch with major customers and understands their changing needs.	Strongly Disagree ☐ ☐ ☐ ☐ ☐ ☐	Strongly Agree	N/A ☐
58	Seeks to understand customers' issues, both internal & external, and conveys it to the relevant functions.	Strongly Disagree ☐ ☐ ☐ ☐ ☐ ☐	Strongly Agree	N/A ☐
59	Motivates his/her people to go beyond their call of duty to delight the customers.	Strongly Disagree ☐ ☐ ☐ ☐ ☐ ☐	Strongly Agree	N/A ☐
60	Gathers and analyzes customers' feedback to assist in decision making.	Strongly Disagree ☐ ☐ ☐ ☐ ☐ ☐	Strongly Agree	N/A ☐
61	Ensures deadlines are met for delivery of products or service to clients.	Strongly Disagree ☐ ☐ ☐ ☐ ☐ ☐	Strongly Agree	N/A ☐
62	Ensures that the first item on the agenda in all his meetings is the "customer."	Strongly Disagree ☐ ☐ ☐ ☐ ☐ ☐	Strongly Agree	N/A ☐

IV. SELF-MANAGEMENT

IV.a. Planning and Organizing

63	Sets challenging targets for self even after having achieved significant success.	Strongly Disagree ☐ ☐ ☐ ☐ ☐ ☐	Strongly Agree	N/A ☐
64	Is focused on results and outcome (rather than on activities).	Strongly Disagree ☐ ☐ ☐ ☐ ☐ ☐	Strongly Agree	N/A ☐
65	Able to pursue goals with commitment, passion, and energy.	Strongly Disagree ☐ ☐ ☐ ☐ ☐ ☐	Strongly Agree	N/A ☐

66	Capable of prioritizing multiple demands, uses tasks and resources appropriately, stays focused.	Strongly Disagree ☐ ☐ ☐ ☐ ☐ ☐ Strongly Agree	N/A ☐
67	Creates plans with clear objectives and/or measurable goals to meet performance targets.	Strongly Disagree ☐ ☐ ☐ ☐ ☐ ☐ Strongly Agree	N/A ☐

IV.b. Decision Making, Problem-Solving, and Risk Taking

68	Takes decisions instead of escalating them up to the higher-ups.	Strongly Disagree ☐ ☐ ☐ ☐ ☐ ☐ Strongly Agree	N/A ☐
69	Takes decisions based on logical assumptions, facts, available resources, constraints, & organizational values.	Strongly Disagree ☐ ☐ ☐ ☐ ☐ ☐ Strongly Agree	N/A ☐
70	Makes decisions in a frequently changing and uncertain environment.	Strongly Disagree ☐ ☐ ☐ ☐ ☐ ☐ Strongly Agree	N/A ☐
71	Demonstrates receptiveness toward alternative solutions.	Strongly Disagree ☐ ☐ ☐ ☐ ☐ ☐ Strongly Agree	N/A ☐
72	Fair and compassionate yet willing to make difficult decisions.	Strongly Disagree ☐ ☐ ☐ ☐ ☐ ☐ Strongly Agree	N/A ☐
73	Before taking a reasoned risk, prepares a fallback position to limit any possible negative consequences.	Strongly Disagree ☐ ☐ ☐ ☐ ☐ ☐ Strongly Agree	N/A ☐

IV.c. Business and Commercial Acumen

74	Understands and works toward the company's bottom line.	Strongly Disagree ☐ ☐ ☐ ☐ ☐ ☐ Strongly Agree	N/A ☐
75	Never loses sight of commercial impact of actions.	Strongly Disagree ☐ ☐ ☐ ☐ ☐ ☐ Strongly Agree	N/A ☐

76	Is aware of how his/her area contributes financially to the overall business.	Strongly Disagree ☐ ☐ ☐ ☐ ☐ ☐ Strongly Agree	N/A ☐
77	Absorbs numerical/financial information easily.	Strongly Disagree ☐ ☐ ☐ ☐ ☐ ☐ Strongly Agree	N/A ☐
78	Spots and converts opportunities to an organization's commercial advantage within his/her area.	Strongly Disagree ☐ ☐ ☐ ☐ ☐ ☐ Strongly Agree	N/A ☐

Feedback PART–II:
(Not to be filled by assessee for Self)

CONTINUE	Three things you appreciate about the appraisee's leadership and managerial style, which he/she should continue doing for enhancing Business Performance
	1
	2
	3

STOP	Three things you do not like about the appraisee's leadership and managerial style, which he/she should stop doing for enhancing Business Performance
	1
	2
	3

	Three things you feel about the appraisee's leadership and managerial style, which he/she should start doing for enhancing Business Performance
START	1
	2
	3

Annexure 10.2: A Sample Report of 360 Feedback: Item-wise Summary Result

II. LEADING AND MANAGING PEOPLE
II.d. Performance Orientation

Overall Average Score (out of 6)

Self	6.00
Superior	4.25
Peer/Int. Cust.	4.78
Subordinate	5.08

Subordinate

Peer/Int. Cust.

Superior

Self

1.00 2.00 3.00 4.00 5.00 6.00

Average Scores

Statements	Self	Superiors	Peer/Int. Cust.	Subordinates	All Observers
Monitors performance of subordinates against agreed targets and encourages them to take corrective actions	6.00	4.50	4.86	5.00	4.83
Proactively ensures that people improve their performance	6.00	3.50	4.63	5.33	4.62
Facilitates people to perform as per role expectation	6.00	4.50	4.63	4.67	4.62
Recognizes people's performance achievement when they do well.	6.00	4.50	5.00	5.33	5.00

Annexure 10.3: A Sample Developmental Planning Worksheet

Specific developmental goal:

Expected Outcome

What will be different?
How will my organization or work group benefit?
What will I gain by achieving the goal and participation in the process?

Strategies for Development

Strategies	Specific Actions

Obstacles I might face while implementing the strategies

What I will have to give up?
What obstacles or difficulties may exist? How will I manage them?

CHAPTER 11

Measuring Corporate Coaching Effectiveness

When a corporate coach undertakes coaching assignment in an organization, there are certain broad deliverables decided jointly by the organization and the corporate coach. In the beginning of coaching journey, the coach and the executive jointly identify the developmental agenda that are important for the executive. Though it is not generally only on areas of improvement in bottom lines or workplace performance improvement, it is expected that any change of behavior or improvement of skills or change of perspectives of the executive would impact the performance of the executive, which in turn would impact organizational performance. At the end of the coaching, the Human Resource department would like to know whether the deliverables of coaching are achieved as decided before the coaching. They would also like to know how the effectiveness of the individual coach is to be assessed. Coaching effectiveness measurement is therefore essential not only for assessing the impact of any corporate coaching initiative but also the evaluation of individual coaches involved in the intervention.

Any corporate coaching intervention, whether it is executive coaching or behavioral coaching or even internal coaching program, runs for a minimum of nine months to several months. It costs to the organization anything between ₹3 lakhs and 20 lakhs ($6,000 to $40,000) per executive/employee. It is quite obvious that organizations would like to know whether such expenses are justified and the coaching has achieved what it was expected to achieve. In other words, organizations would like to know what are the reasonable returns of their investment, directly or indirectly. Hence, it is important to measure the effectiveness of coaching to justify that the investment made in coaching is not only worth but also most effective for the organization as compared to other developmental initiatives.

It is an already established fact that corporate coaching intervention not only benefits the individual who undergoes coaching but also the organization, which gets direct and indirect benefits in terms of improvement of performance in the workplace of the executives. Whether it is executive coaching or performance coaching or behavioral coaching, the ultimate objective of measuring effectiveness of any corporate coaching initiative is how the change is impacting the organizational performance.

McGovern et al. (2001) postulate that:

1. Coaching translates into doing.
2. Doing translates into impacting the business.
3. This impact can be quantified and maximized.

However, there are many challenges in measuring the effectiveness of corporate coaching interventions. The foremost being there is no clarity at the beginning of the coaching journey on what are the deliverables expected from the coaching. This is because the agenda of the coaching (i.e., personal developmental plan of the executive) is very sketchy or abstract, which gets clarified as the coaching progresses. Sometimes it is not easy to convert intangible expectations from the coaching into tangible goals in corporate coaching. It also takes quite a lot of time and effort for the coach to understand where the executive is now, where he would like to reach, and how this change can be quantified.

Second, the coaching is delivered typically over a long period of time, generally one year or more. By that time, many changes happen in the business, in the organization as well as in the context of the executive. It becomes difficult to isolate external factors in the measurement of outcomes from the coaching.

Third, the most important challenge in the measurement of coaching effectiveness is that coaching deals both with transactional and transformational issues (or it could be tangible and intangible outcomes) of the executive/employee. Though proper measurement matrices can be developed to measure improvement in transactional parameters, it is difficult to develop measurement criteria of transformational issues of the executive, since these issues are quite complex and abstract. For example, issues such as delegation, change of attitudes or perspective, improvement of work-life balance, etc., are some of the areas where difficulties are faced in developing measurement matrices.

The next challenge is that the coaching outcomes are dependent on the coachability of the executive/employee. The role of the coach is only to facilitate the process and help the executive in the change process. The final coaching outcomes will depend on how much the executive is ready to change and there is a will to change. Now, the coachability of each executive/employee is difficult to factor in the measurement of coaching effectiveness.

Finally each coaching assignment is different, each coach follows his/her unique style and approach as well as each executive/employee brings unique coaching challenges in the journey. Now, we discuss how the coaching effectiveness measurement takes into considerations of all these variables.

Donald Kirkpatrick developed the training evaluation model in 1959, known as Kirkpatrick's Model of Evaluation. The Kirkpatrick model is widely used in evaluating the effectiveness of training and development programs in organizations to assess the impact of training on the final outcomes at the workplace in terms of learning, transfer of learning in the work area as well as its impact on the results. In the Kirkpatrick model of training evaluation, there are four levels of evaluation (Kirkpatrick, 1983). These are discussed in the following paragraphs.

Level 1 evaluation is known as "Reaction," i.e., it measures the reactions of the participants immediately after the program. The participants' thoughts and feelings about the training or learning experience just after attending the program are collected. It is also called a "Smile Sheet" or "Happy Sheet" feedback. It covers how participants felt about the trainers, the subject matter, the facilities, the food, logistics arrangements, training infrastructure and environment, etc.

Level 2 evaluation focuses on the "Learning." Learning can be defined as attitudes and/or behaviors that were changed, and knowledge and skills that were learned. It does not include application of learning at workplace. Level 2 evaluation aims at the assessment of what the participants learned from the training. Did the participants learn anything? Did the program meet the learning objectives? Whether there is any increase in knowledge, skills, or abilities or change in attitudes or behavior of the participants resulted after attending the training program? Can this be objectively verified by evaluation before and after the training event? Does the participant demonstrate mastery of the subject as intended by the learning objectives after attending the program? This evaluation is done based on criterion-referenced testing. However, it is still not clear whether the participants are using their new learning at their place of work.

Level 3 evaluation focuses on transfer of knowledge, skills, and attitudes from classroom to the job. Five requirements must be met for change of behavior to occur (Kirkpatrick, 1987):

1. Desire to change
2. Knowhow of what to do and how to do it
3. The right job climate
4. Help in applying the classroom learning
5. Rewards for changing behavior

There are several approaches for level 3 evaluation. One approach could be to observe or test the executive/employee after six months or one year to see to what extent the executives/employees are applying their learned skills at their workplace. In the case of change of attitude or behavior change, 360-degree feedback is an important assessment tool.

Level 4 evaluation focuses on results. The impact of any training program can be stated in terms of results such as improvement of productivity, less rejection, improvement of quality, improvement of customer satisfaction, reduction of employee turnover, etc. It actually measures the bottom-line impact on the organization after six months to one year after the employee attended the training program. Since there are many complicating factors in the measurement of results, it is difficult to measure business results accurately. Some of the skill-oriented programs are easy to measure as compared to change of attitudes and behaviors and its impact in the business result.

Philips (1997) introduced the level 5 of evaluation, which is Return on Investment (ROI). It measures the relationship of the monetary value of the results and the cost incurred directly or indirectly for the training initiative. ROI is calculated as follows:

$$ROI = (Benefits–Cost) \times 100/Cost$$

Kirkpatrick's model of training evaluation can be used in measuring the effectiveness of corporate coaching intervention.

Level 1: What are the immediate reactions of the executive/employee just completing the coaching journey? What they liked or did not like? What he felt about the coach?

Annexure 11.1 gives one such evaluation format, which can be administered to the executive at the end of the coaching journey.

Level 2: What are new things the executive/employee learnt from the coaching? What are skills he learned, what new perspectives he acquired, or what new knowledge he acquired during the coaching journey?

Annexure 11.2 gives an example of evaluation of coaching effectiveness at the learning level.

Level 3: What new skills, knowledge, new perspectives, or attitudes gained from the coaching have been applied by the executive/employee at his/her personal life and work-life? What are the evidences available to measure that the employee is deploying new skills or new behavior in effective and meaningful ways? One approach could be to conduct 360-degree feedback assessment before and after the coaching using the same questionnaire.

Annexure 11.3 presents a simple format that can be used to assess if there is any change observed at the workplace of the executive after the executive has undergone the coaching program. This assessment can be done by the reporting officer of the executive and/or peers.

Level 4: How the coaching has impacted the business result? What measurement matrices can be used to measure the impact of coaching in improving business results and can be attributed only to coaching and not to other parameters. Examples given in the following case examples are useful in level 4 evaluation. It is important here to note that many external factors are responsible for business results. Therefore, specific metrics need to be identified on which coaching effectiveness on results will be evaluated. Some of the examples could be sales number, new customer added, productivity index, manufacturing cost, downtime reduction, employee satisfaction index or engagement score, customer satisfaction index, employee turnover percentage, etc.

Some examples of measurement of corporate coaching effectiveness are given below.

Case Example 1

In early 2001, Manchester Consulting Inc. conducted level 4 assessment of 100 executives from Fortune 1,000 companies, who underwent coaching and reported the following tangible improvement for the companies (McGovern et al., 2001) by the frequency of responses of impact reported by executives:

1. Productivity (reported by 53 percent executives)
2. Quality (48 percent)
3. Organizational strength (48 percent)
4. Customer service (39 percent)
5. Reducing customer complaints (34 percent)
6. Retaining executives who received coaching (32 percent)
7. Cost reductions (23 percent)
8. Bottom-line profitability (22 percent)

Contd.

Contd.

Intangible benefits reported are:

9. Improved working relationship with direct reports (77 percent executives)
10. Improved working relationship with immediate supervisors (71 percent)
11. Improved teamwork (67 percent)
12. Improved working relationship with peers (63 percent)
13. Improved job satisfaction (61 percent)
14. Reduced conflict (52 percent)
15. Increased organizational commitment (44 percent)
16. Improved working relationship with executives (37 percent)
17. Other intangibles (31 percent)

Case Example 2

Executive M was working in a multinational organization, based at Europe and posted at India operation as General Manager. He was number two in the organizational hierarchy in India operation. Before coming to India, he was working in system department at headquarter, not having much exposure in international operation.

He was identified by the group as high-potential manager. This organization initiated a talent development program for high-potential managers across various locations across the world. In the talent development program, each participant underwent classroom sessions once in a quarter for four quarters at the headquarter, besides working on specific projects. To measure coaching effectiveness, this organization used two psychometric tools. One was 360-degree feedback survey and the other was EQ-i. Both the tools were administrated to each participant before the coaching journey and at the end of the coaching journey.

As a part of the talent management program, each participant was assigned an executive coach, who worked with the executive on a one-to-one basis for nine months on the developmental areas emerged from the assessment tools.

Table 11.1 gives the comparison of EQ-i score before and after coaching sessions of one such executive. This table reflects clearly that coaching helped this executive improve his emotional and social skills.

Contd.

Contd.

Table 11.1 Coaching Effectiveness Assessment through EQ-i Scores

Score Summary	Before Coaching	After Coaching
Total EQ	91	98
INTRAPERSONAL	90	98
Self-regard	85	88
Emotional self-awareness	77	80
Assertiveness	104	115
Independence	96	109
Self-actualization	100	112
INTERPERSONAL	78	84
Empathy	72	76
Social responsibility	69	75
Interpersonal relationship	94	94
STRESS MANAGEMENT	96	103
Stress tolerance	97	103
Impulse control	96	101
ADAPTABILITY	101	102
Reality testing	95	96
Flexibility	92	98
Problem solving	117	114
GENERAL MOOD	101	103
Optimism	97	108
Happiness	105	101

Level 5: Recently, some organizations started exploring the measurement of coaching effectiveness in terms of Return on Investment (ROI) of coaching, since the investment in some cases go to many million dollars. In ROI calculation, there are two components: Benefits and Cost. Benefits, i.e., the results, are calculated in financial terms by the organization. However, it is very difficult to measure benefits, which are only from coaching not from other

factors. McGovern et al. (2001) are the first to undertake a study to measure the impact of executive coaching using ROI. To isolate the effects of coaching from other factors, benefits estimates were multiplied by the percent of the improvement that the executive attributed to coaching, called the isolation factor. To adjust the potential errors in estimation, benefit estimates were multiplied by the executive confidence level in their benefits (results) estimated. Based on adjusted benefits, ROI is then calculated.

The cost includes expenses on payment to coaches, assessment charges, and other administrative expenses for the delivery of coaching. A very few organizations are evaluating coaching effectiveness using ROI as of now.

Chapter Summary

Measurement of corporate coaching effectiveness is one of the critical areas of coaching, since organizations spent considerable amount of money for coaching interventions, besides time and efforts. Organizations are therefore interested to know what are the impacts of such investment and how it can be established that the coaching had delivered what it is expected to deliver. The Kirkpatrick model of training evaluation can be used to measure coaching effectiveness. Level 1 evaluation measures the reaction of executives just after they complete the coaching. Level 2 evaluation focuses on learning of the executive during the coaching journey. Level 3 evaluation looks for evidence to ensure that the executives have deployed their learning in the workplace. Level 4 evaluation of coaching effectiveness measures the impact of coaching on the results derived by the organization.

Annexure 11.1: Coaching Effectiveness Evaluation (Level 1)

Your Name: Coach Name:

Dates during which   Number of Coaching
you got coaching: sessions:

1. How do you rate the overall coaching program?
   a. Excellent
   b. Very good
   c. Good
   d. Average
   e. Poor
2. To what extent this coaching will help you?
   a. To a large extent
   b. To some extent
   c. Very little
3. How you will rate your coach?
   a. Excellent
   b. Very good
   c. Good
   d. Average
   e. Poor
4. How much you could achieve your coaching goals?
   a. To a large extent
   b. To some extent
   c. Not at all
5. Do you think the coaching will help you in improvement of your leadership/managerial/supervisory skills?
   a. To a large extent
   b. To some extent
   c. Not much

6. What you think this coaching will help you in improvement of performance at your work area?
   a. To a large extent
   b. To some extent
   c. Not much
   d. Not sure
7. Does coaching help you gain new perspectives/ideas/ thoughts?
   a. Yes
   b. No
8. How do you rate your satisfaction from the coaching experience?
   a. Very much satisfied
   b. Satisfied
   c. Satisfied to some extent
   d. Not satisfied

Annexure 11.2: Coaching Effectiveness Evaluation (Level 2)

Your Name: Coach Name:

Dates during which   Number of Coaching
you got coaching: sessions:

1. Coaching helped me gain new knowledge, skills, and abilities.
   a. Strongly agree
   b. Agree to a large extent
   c. Agree
   d. Disagree to some extent
   e. Strongly disagree

If your answer to previous question is (a) to (c), please reply the following questions:

2. Please identify in which areas you have gained your knowledge, which will be helpful in your work.

3. Please identify at least two work-related skills you have gained as a result of coaching.

4. Please identify new perspective/insight you have got from the coaching.

5. What are the areas you could transfer your new knowledge, skills, or insights? Please identify at least two areas of transfer.

6. How you rate your overall learning as a result of coaching?
   a. Excellent
   b. Very good
   c. Good
   d. Fair
   e. Poor

Annexure 11.3: Coaching Effectiveness Evaluation (Level 3)

Name of the Executive (Executive):

Duration of Coaching:

Your Name:

Your Relationship with Executive:

Please give your feedback on what are the changes you have observed after this executive underwent coaching:

Areas	Significant Change	Good Visible Change	Moderate Change	Some Change	No Change
Dealing with subordinates					
Dealing with seniors					
Dealing with peers					
Ability to manage team					
Ability to manage performance					
Ability to communicate and listen					
Ability to manage himself					
Ability to meet performance expectations					

References

Kirkpatrick, D. (1987). Evaluation. In R.L. Craig (ed.), *Training and development handbook*, pp. 301–319. New York: McGraw-Hill Book Company.

Kirkpatrick, D.L. (1983). Four steps to measuring training effectiveness. *Personnel Administrators*, 28 (11), pp. 19–25.

McGovern, J., Lindermann, M., Vengara, M., Murphy, S., Barker, L., & Warrenfeltz, R. (2001). Maximizing the impact of executive coaching: Behavioral change, organizational outcomes and returns of investment. *The Manchester Review*, 6 (1), pp. 1–9.

Philips, J.J. (1997). *Return on investment in training and performance improvement programs*. Houston, Texas: Gulf Publishing Company.

Index

About the Author

Sraban Mukherjee, CPC, PCC (ICF) is an executive coach who specializes in the area of behavioral coaching. Dr Mukherjee splits his professional time between executive coaching and strategic human resources. He has around 30 years of professional experience in large corporations in India where he headed the Human Resource function, and handled various critical HR assignments at business and corporate strategic level. He specializes in people development interventions, OD, and leadership skill enhancement domain and deals with both transactional and transformational issues in coaching process.

Dr Mukherjee has worked closely with board level and leadership level executives on coaching and development areas. He has coached clients across the globe ranging from business issues to breakthrough performance issues and leadership effectiveness areas. His clients include senior executives and high potential managers of ONGC, NTPC, ONIDA, Alcatel-Lucent, Seco Tools, Thomson Press, Insta Group, National Hydro-Power Corporation, Grasim Industries, JSW Steels, Shree Cement, and other organizations.

He has also conducted several competency development centers for senior and middle management, internal coach development program, coaching skill training and leadership development interventions for large corporations.

Dr Mukherjee is an engineer by basic education and PhD from the Indian Institute of Technology, Delhi. He graduated in Coaching from ACTP program of ICF. In his coaching practice, he has emphasized the use of behavioral methodologies including methods used by Marshall Goldsmith. He is a trained assessor for individual and organizational assessment, and qualified for the administration of MBTI. He is licensed for the administration of

DISC. He is also certified for EQ-I 2.0 and EQ360 (Emotional intelligence) tools.

Dr Mukherjee has published several action research papers in peer reviewed sections of leading international coaching journals, viz., *International Journal of Evidence based Coaching and Mentoring, European Journal of Mentoring and Coaching, International Journal of Coaching in Organization*, etc. He is a member of International Editorial Board of *International Journal of Coaching: Theory, Research and Practice*. His coaching model, the Delta Coaching Model, was reported at Canada and Australia. He has been quoted several times by leading newspapers and magazines in coaching- and HR-related articles. He is a Professional Certified Coach (PCC) of ICF, USA.

Dr Mukherjee believes that every coaching relation results into change of behavior and hence his coaching primarily focuses on behavioral change during coaching journey. His coaching niche is in corporate and business coaching.